P9-CQX-712

NUMBER 661

THE ENGLISH EXPERIENCE

ITS RECORD IN EARLY PRINTED BOOKS
PUBLISHED IN FACSIMILE

GEORGE GIFFORD

A PLAINE DECLARATION THAT OUR BROWNISTS BE DONATISTS

LONDON, 1590

WALTER J. JOHNSON, INC.
THEATRUM ORBIS TERRARUM, LTD.
AMSTERDAM 1974 NORWOOD, N.J.

The publishers acknowledge their gratitude to
the Master and Fellows of Emmanuel College,
Cambridge for their permission to reproduce
the Library's copy, Shelfmark: 32.2.56(5)

S.T.C. No. 11862

Collation: $*^4$, A-R^4

Published in 1974 by

Theatrum Orbis Terrarum, Ltd.
O.Z. Voorburgwal 85, Amsterdam

&

Walter J. Johnson, Inc.
355 Chestnut Street
Norwood, New Jersey
07648

Printed in the Netherlands

ISBN 90 221 0661 6

Library of Congress Catalog Card Number:
74-80180

A
Plaine Declaration

that our *Brownists* be full *Donatists*, *by comparing them together* from point to point out of the writings of Augustine.

Also a replie to Master Greenwood *touching* read prayer, wherein his grosse ignorance is detected, which labouring to purge himselfe from former absurdities, doth plunge himselfe deeper into the mire.

By George Gyffard *Minister of Gods word in* Maldon.

AT LONDON,
Printed for *Toby Cooke*, dwelling at the Tygers head in Paules Churchyard. 1590.

TO THE RIGHT HONORABLE, SIR *William Cecill*, Knight *of the Garter, Baron of* Burghley, *Lord* high Treasurer of *England*, and Chauncellor *of the Vniuersitie of* Cambridge: *Grace and peace.*

I *Published a Booke (Right Honourable) against the* Brownists, *who complaine of hard dealing, and not onlie they, but others, in that I haue termed them* Donatists, *and charge them with sundrie foule matters. And hauing now receiued from them an answer vnto one part of that my booke; I haue also framed this replie: In which I first set downe from point to point out of the writings of the holie Father* Augustine, *with what Scriptures and arguments it was defended, and so compare our mens writings and doings with the same. They must for this, chuse either to affirme, that the* Donatists *had the truth, and the chur-*

ches were perished: or else shewe some materiall points of Donatisme, *which they doo not hold. And then in the latter part of this my booke, I answer to that which is published now by them against read prayer. As I was bold to present the former unto your Honor, so do I also humblie offer this, presuming upon your Honors fauourable acceptation. And thus I beseech the Lord God to blesse and prosper your Honor.*

Amen.

To the Reader.

GOod Christian reader, I published a booke against the *Brownists*, whom I haue in the same termed the *Donatists* of *England*. How farre of I was from purposing anie such thing at the first, and how I was drawne into it afterward, I haue in that former booke truly reported. And for warrant of my doing before the Lord, I had no doubt but that it should bee an acceptable seruice to Christ: notwithstanding when I respect the waightines and necessitie of the worke, I haue alwaies wished, and do wish, that some man of greater learning might deale against thẽ. Neither as yet am I cast into any thoughts of doubting, by the mislike, or fault finding of some in all places, which are no *Brownists*: But I am rather thrust forward by beholding that weakenes of iudgement and want of vnderstanding not in a feaw, touching the foulnes of *Donatisme*, and by the sight of such nerenes of multitudes vnto the danger, which before I coulde not suspect. Now touching the faultes which are found, which causeth the mislike, they are partelie for the matter it selfe, and partlie for the manner of dealing both in it, as also towards the persons themselues against whome I write. In the matter some haue found fault as though I should stand to cleere & to iustifie al things, not onlie in the Booke of Common praier, but also in the calling and ordination of our Ministers, and in our

Church gouernement, others affirme that I haue diminished the faults which are esteemed to be in these, and made them lighter, at the least by not reproouing them. The first sort I cannot but meruaile at, seeing I haue in that my former booke set downe expresslie in these words, that the matter in question betweene the *Brownists* and me, is not about the controuersie in our Church, as whether there be imperfections, corruptions and faults, in our Worship, Ministerie and Church gouernement, nor how many great or smal: but whether there be such heinous enormities as destroy the verie life, and being of a true Church, and make an vtter diuorse from Christ. I doo then lay open the state of this question so plainelie, as I know not how to make it more plaine: now vnles I should run through euerie particular which wee deale in, which I thought to be needlesse, but now I will a litle stand vpon it. They reckon Romish fasts, Ember dayes, Saincts eues and Lent: Idoll feasts, as Alhallowes, Candlemas, seuerall Ladie daies, Saincts daies, dedicating Churches vnto Saints. Comminations, Rogations, and Purifications, Tithes, Offerings, Mortuaries, howsling the sick, with the Sacrament, absolution, and blasphemous dirges, and funerall Sermons, ouer and for the dead. Corrupt manner of administring the Sacraments, the Font, the crosse in Baptisme, Baptisme by women, gossippings, blasphemous and hereticall collects. These and certaine other haue they set downe, to bee in the Booke not vnder the termes of faults, blemishes and corruptions, but as heresies, blasphemies, and abominations, and that such as ouerturne the foundation of the

Christian

Christian faith, destroy the substance of Gods worship, and take away the life, and beeing of a true Church. To this I haue answered, that they be foule slaunderours liars, & false accusers, shewing that our Church hath renounced in those former things that which is blasphemous and hereticall, or so abominable, as that it approacheth neerest to the destroying of the faith and holy worship of the Lord. As namelie the remission of sinnes, and merite of eternall life by fasting, which is the doctrine of the Romish church. The worship and inuocation of Saints and Angels, the power of expelling Diuels by the signe of the crosse, and such like things which the papacie is full of, but reiected by vs. If the *Brownists* in their replie against that I haue written, shall prooue by the word of God, that there be great corruptiõs in our praiers, in our fasts, in our keeping the Saints dayes, in the Crosse, and in manie other things which bee in our Church, as in our Ministerie and Church gouernemẽt. And further if their proofes be neuer so clere & strong from the Scriptures, yet they answere not me at al, nor touch the question or controuersie between them and me, vnles they can prooue them to be such faults as destroy the worship of God, ouerturne the foundation of the faith, and take away the verie life and being of true Christianitie. If (I say) they do not prooue them, according as they haue set thẽ downe, to bee blasphemies, heresies, abominations, yea the verie worship and yoake of Antichrist, the marke of the beast, and his power: I remaine vnanswered, and they stand conuicted as liars, slanderers and most wicked false accusers not of particular persons, but of

whole

whole Churches. For I ſhewed in expreſſe wordes that I doo not meddle at all in theſe queſtions, whether there bee corruptions and faults in our Church condemned by Gods word, whether they bee manie or fewe, whether they bee ſmall or great, but onelie thus farre whether they bee ſuch or ſo great, as make our Churches Antichriſtian. Here therefore I doo intreate the Chriſtian Reader to fixe his eyes in reading my writings and theirs, onelie vppon this one queſtion, whether there be in our Church any errors or faults that be found amentall? Looke if I haue in this point by denying that there bee ſwarued from the ſacred word of God, from the iudgement of the holie Churches, and writings of the moſt worthy & noble inſtruments which God hath at all times giuen to be the guides and lights in the ſame. And if it can be prooued, that I haue gone awrie from the trueth but an heare breadth, I will reuoke it: for trueth is to bee bowed vnto and reuerenced, whereſoeuer ſhee ſheweth her ſweete face, of all that looke to haue any part in her. Marke alſo their writings as they ſhall come foorth, and ſee wherein they can conuince me of any error, falſehood or corruption, touching this one forenamed queſtion, vnto which they are to be held ſeeing we ſet all other controuerſies aſide.

Then touching the ſecond ſorte, which finde fault about handling the matter, as if that I ſhould mitigate or make lighter the faults of our Churches, at leaſt in this, that I do not reprehend them. To this I anſwer, firſt, that vnles it can bee ſhewed, that our Church is guilty in ſome of thoſe crimes which I ſtand to clere it in, I ſee no reaſon why I ſhoulde bee charged to

make

make things lighter, which I medle not withall, further than in shewing that they be not fundamentall. Secondlie, I intreate al men to consider that I stand to defend a Church, and not the infirmities or offences of a Church, in which as there be many bad mēbers, so the best are fraile. If a godlie man because of some apparant sinnes, should be accused to be an Atheist, an infidell, a traitor, or a most vile and filthie wretch: might not he clere himselfe of such horrible crimes, but it must be saide, he dooth mittigate his owne infirmities or make them lighter? Thirdlie, I doo request them to consider the state of our people, how speedelie verie manie are carried into great euils and dangers, though not all in the same degree. I am of this minde, that where any thing is amisse in Gods Church, it is the part and duetie of the faithfull Ministers of Christ, all dutifull reuerence and submission being obserued towards Magistrates & publique authoritie, peaciblie to seeke redresse of the same, with godlie and charitable reprehension. I doo also holde that euery christian man is wiselie and soberly (with the like dueties of reuerence, submission, and peaceable behauiour obserued) to seeke to haue his conscience informed in all matters, which may any way concerne himselfe. But we see how farre some haue swarued and doo swarue from this. For the rule of charitie and christian dueties being neglected, the vtter disgrace and contempt of men is sought, and that on either part. The warre is made as deadlie, as if the grounds of christianitie were in question: while some passing the bounds of modestie, others doo replie against them after the same manner. Our Sauiour saith Satan dooth not cast foorth Satan. and shall we thinke then that sinne, shall cast foorth sinne? Such as condemne and abhorre Schisme and errors, and inordinate dealing, must bee burthened and reproached with the same notwithstanding, which is iniurious. And what is in the mouthes of many against this, but that the Papists then may as well be excused, which condemne Master *Luther* and other as the fathers of heretiks, because swarmes of Anabaptists did followe immediatelie vpon their preaching the Gospel? When shall we then here come to an end? There wil bee contention in the Church: and humaine frailtie hath shewed it selfe this way, euen among the holie teachers of old, to the sharp reprehension, and in manner reproaching one of another, as Master *Beza* noteth in the Epistle of his Booke against *Erastus*: but godlie men when they haue somewhat gone awrie, seek to amend their fault, by subduing their passions. Now looke also vpon the people, where wee may see verie many; who not regarding the chiefe christian vertues & godlie dueties, as namelie to be meek, to be patient, to be lowlie, to be full of loue and mercie, to deale vprightlie and iustly, to guide their families in the feare of God, with wholsome instructions, and to stand fast in the calling, in which God hath set them) giue thẽselues wholy to this, euen as if it were the summe and pith of religion, namelie to argue and talke continuallie against matters in the Church, against Bishops and Ministers, and one against another on both sides. Some are proceeded to this, that they will come to the assemblies to heare the Sermons and praiers of the Preacher, but not to the praiers of the booke, which I take to be a more grieuous sinne than manie doo suppose. But yet this is not the worst, for

sundry

ſundrie are gone further, and fallen into a damnable Schiſme: and the ſame ſo much the more feareful & dangerous, in that manie do not ſee the foulenes of it, but rather holde them as godlie Chriſtians, and but a little ouerſhot in ſome matters. The ſore is grieuous, and the wound is deepe; as I haue ſmall ioy to behold it, ſo haue I leſſe deſire to make it deeper, wiſhing from my heart, that it might rather be cured. Such as bee of another minde, either in this, or in any thing that I haue writtẽ, I craue of them, that they wil giue me leaue, according to the doctrine and rule of the Apoſtle, *fraterne diſſentire*, to diſſent in ſome thing, without the breach and hindrance of brotherly loue. For as I do greatlie eſteeme that rule of S. *Paul*, let as manie as be perfect be thus minded: if any be otherwiſe minded, God will reueale it. But ſo farre as we are come, let vs proceed by one rule, to be like affectioned *Phil.*3. ſo do I much lament to ſee it almoſt vtterly neglected, and the breach of loue & concord as violent among many, for euery matter wherein they diſſent, as if ſome ground of chriſtianity were in queſtion between them. I do not meane that a man ought to conſent vnto any error, or vnto any euill committed by others, or to neglect the inſtructing and admoniſhing, as his place and calling dooth require. But I had rather (as one ſaith) anſwer to God, if I muſt giue account, for mercie, rather than for rigour and ſeueritie. I knowe there be faults in extremities on both ſides: as on the one ſide vnder a perſwaſion of loue, a man may be ouer fauorable in eſteeming and bearing as brethren, ſuch as hold the foundations of the faith, and yet erre in ſome things, and haue great faultes: ſo on the other ſide, vnder a perſwaſion of zeale againſt all falsehood and wickednes, they may fall into an vncharitable rigour, as very many doo. The nature of man is more prone to this latter, and the fall is more grieuous than in that former; few are carried with aboundance of godly loue, to offend in ouer fauorable judging their brethren: and because the elect of God haue great infirmities, & the Scripture doth not warrant men to be rigorous in condemning, if a man holding the hatred & zeale against all sin, iudge & repute them as christian brethren, which it may be are not, his fall is not great, although he be ouer fauourable; for through humility he is below. Wheras on the other part, such as condemne with vncharitable rigor, they are lifted vp with swelling, and so their fall is deeper. This is my meaning in that I saide, I had rather answer to God for mercy than for rigour: now as I eschew it in my self, so would I be loath, seeing rigor aboundeth among many, to giue any occasion to nourish the same by my writing. If I sin in this, yet I trust it is so, as no godly charitable man & wel aduised wil make an outcry against me for it; if I shake hāds with sin let me be condēned for it, otherwise I craue that I may follow the rule of the Apostle. But now it wil be said by the third sort which finde fault with my book that I haue broken this rule towards the *Brownists*: as also that rule of S. *Paul*, who willeth to instruct with patience such as be contrary minded, because I charg them not only with foule Schisme, but also with heresies, and for which I take it that obstinacie if it be found in thē, wil make them heretickes. They differ not frō vs, say some, in matters of faith, but doo ouer shoot thēselues, & that on the right hand: for answer vnto these, first touching the rules of *Paul*, I know he himselfe

himselfe did practize thẽ. And he that gaue these rules, so far as wee are come let vs proceed by one rule, &c. and instructing with patience &c. said also beware of dogs, beware of euill workmen, beware of the concision. *Philip.*3.

Why did S. *Paule* this, but mooued with the danger which the Churches were in by them? Men haue not now the consideration what it is to condemne the whole worship & the Ministrie as Antichristian, and so vtterlie to take away the credite and power of the Ministrie and preaching Gods word. Will they esteeme it to bee lesse than that which the false Apostles did? Againe, I see men are ignorant what the power of *Donatisme* was, how it preuailed and spread not onelie among the common sort, but had hundreths of preachers to publish and set it foorth. Neither doo men knowe the foulenes of *Donatisme*, nor the poynts of it, and that maketh them offended, that I terme the *Brownists Donatists*, & hold it as a schisme and heresie. *Cresconius* the *Donatist* writing against *Augustine*, doth reprehend him for calling them heretickes; because they held the same doctrine, as hee saith, and if they offended, it could bee but as in a schisme. *Augustine* replieth, that *Schisma inueteratum est hæresis*, Inueterate schisme is heresie. And sheweth that some thinges they helde were hereticall. The Churches haue condemned it not only as a schisme, but also as an heresie. I haue out of large discourses of the controuersies betweene the Churches and the *Donatists*, drawen foorth brieflie all the chiefe heads of *Donatisme*, and how they did stand to maintaine them, and with what scriptures. I compare the *Brownists* and them together in all poynts generallie held,

 and

and will ſtand to iuſtifie that they bee full *Donatiſts*, euen in the rankeſt *Donatiſme*. If I haue not ſet down the *Donatiſme* aright, and if the *Browniſme* be not the ſame, let me haue the ſhame for euer, that I haue giuē them the title, and can not iuſtifie that they are worthie of it. Let the *Browniſts* chuſe which part they will, either to affirme that the *Donatiſts* had the truth, or elſe to cleere thēſelues frō *Donatiſme*, I will ioyne with them, or rather againſt them in either. And in the meane time I do exhort al other to be ſober minded and diſcreet, and not to thruſt the ſimpler ſort headlong into it, by exclaiming that they bee ouer hardlie dealt withall. For what ſay ſome? If theſe that are called *Browniſts* bee godly men, and but ouerſeene in ſome matters, we will chuſe to ioyne with thē, rather thā with the publike aſſemblies of our Church. Theſe men are they in compaſsion of whō I write. Now, the chiefe heads in which I compare them are theſe: The *Donatiſts* did falſelie accuſe and condemne the Churches and al the Miniſters to be vtterlie polluted, and al their worſhip, and ſeparated themſelues without all order of diſcipline: So haue the *Browniſts* done. The *Donatiſts* tooke beginning by occaſion of one man, whom they held to be no Miniſter of Chriſt, but after they made their defence that all were polluted, and all the Miniſters the generatiōs of Traitors, Iudaſſes, and perſecutors of the iuſt: that the Churches in the beginning after the times of perſecution were not well ordered by ſeparation of the faithfull from the wicked. For becauſe there were many both Miniſters and people which in time of perſecution to ſaue their liues had denied the faith & ſacrificed to Idols, and deliuered the holie Scriptures to the persecutors: and when *Constantine* gaue peace, being become Christian, returned and were not cast foorth. Hereupon the *Donatists* said all were vtterlie polluted: & that because some such did ordaine Ministers, at least as they reported, they accused all the Ministers to bee the sons of traitors which ordained them, and so were no ministers of Christ, had no true praier, nor Sacraments. The *Brownists* affirme that all our assemblies which openlie committed Idolatrie, were at the sound of a Trumpet, at the coronation of the Queene called to be Churches: that the bad were not separated frõ the good: that our ordainers were Idolaters, & that we are their children; no Ministers of Christ, but Baals priests & persecutors: & so haue no word of God, nor no Sacraments, nor true church, all being polluted with the open sinnes committed. Thus both make the holie things of the Lord, which indeed are vnchangeable, or els we could haue no cõfort: as namely, the word of God, the praiers, the Sacraments, & the ordination of Ministers, to be polluted & destroied by the wickednes of men. The *Donatists* held that Princes were not to compell vnto religion, & so cried out of persecution, & gloried of their sufferings & multitude of martyres. And what do the *Brownists*? These things with the rest will better appeare in the seuerall comparisons, as they followe in my booke. I now intreate the reader not to iudge of any one thing vntill he haue read the whole. I also desire that the sayings of the ancient writers which I alleage may be wel waied, for proofe of that for which I cite them. If any shall say, what shall we ground vppon men? I answer, I alleage them but to shew what the controuersie was & how it was disputed on both

sides:

ſides: & for this they are ſufficient witneſſes. Beleeue their reaſons as ye find they be confirmed by the holie Scriptures: I haue ſet downe the Latin, leaſt any ſhould thinke I haue not dealt plainlie. And touching the laſt part of this my booke which is an anſwer to Maſter *Greenwood*, concerning read prayer, peruſe it throughlie and then iudge whether I haue charged him wrongfullie in any matter. I do lament that many of our people which haue been hearers of the Goſpell, ſhould be ſo ignorant, as to ſuck in ſuch dregs as he offereth. Now to conclude, there are two things which deceiue many, which I deſire thẽ to conſider: one is that they are caried away with many true and notable ſentences of Scripture & worthie principles which the *Browniſts* ſet down, not conſidering or not eſpying how they from them doo draw out falſe aſſumptions, and thereupon cõclude that which is vntrue. The other is that they looke not vpõ that which followeth vppon their wordes by conſequence, but ſtand vpon this, O they hold no ſuch thing, they haue wrong. Maſter *Greenwood* crieth out that he doth not condẽne al Churches, he denieth not that the pſalmes are to be ſung to God, he ſaith not that the regenerate do not ſin, he hath no ſuch meaning, he hath wrong. But mark if I haue done him any wrong at all: looke vpon his ſayings, and vpon that which muſt needes followe vpon them. The other *Browniſts* crie out of the like wrõgs. Iudge not vntil both ye heare wherein they haue wrong, and ſee mine anſwer. If I haue charged them with matter which either their words doo not expreſſe, or that followeth not from them by neceſſarie conſequence, let me then bee iudged raſh and vncharitable.

FINIS.

That the Brownists are full *Donatists.*

O Apostle, no Prophet, no Euangelist, no true pastor or teacher can haue his owne name put vpon the Disciples which he gathereth: but as they bee all gathered onely by Christes doctrine and vnto Christ alone, according as it is written, one is your Doctor, euen Christ: Matth. 23. so are they onely by his title called Christians. But it hath béen the manner of olde, and euen from the time of the Apostles, in Gods Church, when any wicked schisme or heresie hath sprung vp, to call the scholers and followers by the names of the first masters of the same, and chiefe leaders. As of Montanus, the Montanists; of Nouatius, the Nouatians; of Arrius, the Arrians; of Pelagius, the Pelagians; of Donatus, the Donatists; of the Pope, the Papists, &c. And who shall reprehend this as vaine, or condemne it as a thing vniust, seeing wee followe his example, who saith to the Angell of the Church of Pergamus, Reuel. 2. Thou hast them which hold the doctrine of the Nicholaitanes? Now, there is a sect in England commonly called Brownists, not because Browne was the first originall of it, but for that he hath written and published bookes in maintenance and enlargement thereof, and with more skill and learning than others which either as yet haue followed, or gone before him. Many men thinke that they

bee sprung vp but of late, whereas in very déede it is well knowne there was a Church of them in London 20. yeares past, and one Bolton a principall doer therein, whose feare-full end is not forgotten. I haue termed them the Donatists of England. How iustly, and how charitablie, and with what due consideration, it standeth me now vpon to shewe; least the ignoranter sort of such as somewhat fauour them, should imagine, that I haue iniuriouslie and falselie giuen them this odious title, to worke their vniust discredite. For Donatisme in olde time, about twelue hundred yeares past, was condemned as a detestable proud Schisme and heresie, that began at Carthage in Aphrica, and was vehementlie withstood by the faithfull Pastors, and cut downe by the holie Scriptures, as no learned godlie man will denie. The holie Father Augustine was the chiefe that did ouerthrowe them, as his writings which are extant, answering to their writings at large doo declare. Now, my purpose at this time is to compare them together, the Donatists and the Brownists, from point to point out of the writings of Augustine. If it fall out cléere and manifest that they agree together, as euen as two peeces of cloath that are of the same wooll, the same thréed, colour, working & breadth: and that an Egge is no liker to an Egge, than they be each to other: I hope all that be sober minded will not blame me for giuing them the same title. Their originall, first, (of the Donatists I meane, and how they cut off themselues) is to bee noted & set forth; which was this. From the birth of our Sauiour Christ, for the space of thrée hundred yeares & more, there were euer anon great and greeuous persecutions raised vp against the Church, by the Romane Emperours, vntill the Emperour Constantine the great imbraced the holie Gospell, and gaue peace to the Christians. In those daies of persecution, such as through feare, or otherwise, did deliuer to the cruell persecutors, either the bookes of the holie Scriptures, that they might burne and deface them, or the vessells appointed for holie vse in the publike assemblies, that they might carrie them away; or the names of the brethren, that they might

finde

finde them out: such (I say) were called *traditores*, that is, deliuerers or traitors. There was a rumour that such offence had béen by some committed, as no doubt it was by many. Now, as Augustine reporteth in his Psalme against the Donatists, there came certaine Bishops from Numidia vnto Carthage, a famous Citie in Aphrica, to ordeine a Bishop, and found Cæcilianus alreadie ordeined and placed in the Seate: then were they wroth that they could not ordeine. They ioyned together, and layd a crime vpon Cæcilianus. They say his ordeiner deliuered the holie bookes and was a traitor: whereupon they will haue him reputed no Minister of Christ, but the sonne of a traitor. There was no assemblie of the learned Pastors for to iudge in this case according to Christes ordinance and discipline: the accused and the accuser did not stand forth for triall. There were no witnesses produced to proue the crime: neither were matters scanned by the Scriptures. But *furor, dolus, & tumultus*, that is, furie, deceipt, and tumult, did beare the sway, as Augustine sheweth in the same his Psalm. They assembled which were the accusers, and Cæcilianus is condemned being absent, by Tigisitanus Secundus, as hée sheweth in his first booke against Parmenian Chap. 3. and in his third booke against Cresconius Chap. 40. Now was there great stirre and deuision begun: Donatus, he steppeth forth and requireth of the Emperour Constantine to haue Iudges (not of Aphrica, out beyond the seas) to heare the crime which was to be obiected against Cæcilianus. The Emperour appointed that the matter should bee heard at Rome, where Cæcilianus was cléered, and Donatus and his part receiuing repulse appealed, accusing Meltiades then Bishop of Rome, that he was also *traditor*, as Augustine reporteth in his first booke against Parmenian, Chapt. 5. and so they require to haue the cause heard by the Emperour, vnto whom they had appealed: where hauing also the repulse, as false accusers, they say ẏ Emperour was corrupted through fauour. They made a separation from Cæcilianus and those that claue to him. The deuision grewe greater and greater, they had assemblies and Bishops on Donatus part in processe of time in great number. They condemned not only the Church at Carthage, and the neighbour Churches in Aphrica, as guiltie therewith, but all Churches through the world as wrapped together in the guiltines of those Churches of Aphrica. They pronounced them all polluted, uncleane, abominable and utterlie fallen from the Couenant of God, through the pollution of such as had committed sacrilege, and were not seperated. They said there were no Ministers of Christ, no Sacraments, & so no true Church among them, but heapes of wicked polluted sacrilegious persons, whose teachers were all generations of traitors, Iudasses, & persecutors of Gods Saints, and that as many as would bee saued must seperate themselues, and ioyne with the pure selected companie of Donatus. And for these respects they baptized again all such as fell unto them, as not being baptized before, but polluted with a prophane washing. Now, through the shew of burning zeale, and stiffe rigorous seueritie in condemning sinne, and by the vehement outcries which they made that the discipline was not duely executed, in as much as the prophane were mingled together in the assemblies with ye pure, and no seperation made: many of the people not well settled and grounded in the trueth, were terrified and turned unto them, taking them to be most zealous holie men, and the onlie true Church in earth: and with exceeding bitternesse condemned all other as abominable Idolaters and cursed traytors, whose worship God abhorred. It was before the daies of Augustine that this sect began, and in his time was greatlie spread. And when he wrote that it was against all equitie to condemne (as they did at the first) the whole world for the sinne of Cæcilianus, because if he were guiltie, yet the Churches farre off knew not so much, but might rather iudge him cleere, being cleered in iudgement. They maintained the matter to proue that there were no true flocks, nor pastors after another sort: and did affirme, that as the Church of Carthage, and the Churches elsewhere in Aphrica, were fallen from God by the pollution of the sacrilege of Cæci-

lianus

lianus and other: so all other Churches in the world were destroyed by the like sacrileges committed in the daies of persecution by wicked men among them, whose sinnes were open and knowne and no seperation made. For thus speaketh Parmenian a Donatist Bishop, as Augustine doth set it downe in his first booke against him, and third Chapter. *Dicit etiam Parmenianus; hinc probari conscelerātum fuisse orbem terrarum criminibus traditionis, & aliorum sacrilegiorum: quia cum multa talia fuerint tempore persecutionis admissa, nulla propterea facta est in ipsis prouincijs separatio populorum.* That is, Parmenian also saith, that from hence it is prooued, that the world hath been together made wicked, or hainouslie polluted with the crimes of treason and of other sacrileges: because, when many such things were done in the time of persecution, there was no seperation of the people made for the same in the Prouinces. Marke well this saying of Parmenian the Donatist, for it doth expreslie set downe the ground of Donatisme. The words of Petilian another Donatist Bishop, to proue all the Ministers of the Churches to be but successors of traitors (as Augustine doth report them in his second booke against him Chapt. 8.) are many, I will onely recite the chiefe of them. This Petilian hauing before saide, that he which is baptized by one that is dead, his washing doth profite him nothing: then procéedeth to shewe how farre (as he saith) an vnfaithfull traitor may be accompted dead while he liueth. And for this he frameth a comparison betwéene Iudas and the Pastors of the Church, condemning them as the worse. For after he hath set forth that Iudas was an Apostle when he betraied Christ, and spirituallie dead when he had lost the honour of an Apostle: and as it was foretold by David that another should haue his place, so Matthias succéeded him in the Apostleship. He would haue no foole here dispute that Matthias bare away triumph and not iniurie, which by the victorie of Christ, had the spoyle of the traitor. Then he demandeth, how canst thou by this déede challenge to thy selfe the office of a Bishop, being the heire of a more wicked traitor? *Iudas Christum carnalem tradidit, tu spiritualem; furens Euangelium sanctum flammis sacrilegis tradidisti.* Iudas betraied Christ carnal, thou spirituall; being in furie thou hast deliuered the holie Gospell to the fire. *Iudas legislatorem tradidit perfidis: tu quasi eius reliquias legem dei perdendã hominibus tradidisti.* Iudas betraied the lawgiuer to the wicked: thou hast betraied as it were his reliques the lawe of God vnto mẽ to be destroied. *Si hominis mortui testamentũ flammis incenderes, nonne falsarius punireris? quid de te ergo futurum est, qui sanctissimam legem dei iudicis incendisti?* If thou shouldest burne the will of a dead man, shouldest thou not bee punished as a falsifier? what then shall become of thee, which hast burnt the most holie lawe of GOD the Iudge? *Iudam facti vel in morte pœnituit: te non modò non pœnitet, verumetiam nequissimus traditor nobis legem seruantibus, persecutor & carnifex existis.* Iudas repented him of his deed, at least in death: but thou doest not onely not repent, but also being a most wicked traitor, remainest a persecutor and a tormentor of vs that keepe the lawe. Cresconius a Grammarian (one as it seemeth that taught some Grammar schoole) tooke vpon him to write against Augustine in the defence of Petilian, or rather of the whole Donatisme, and he laieth to the charge of Cæcilianus the vnpardonable sinne against the holie Ghost, in betraying the scriptures to the persecutors, vsing this argument: Holie men of God deliuered them as they were led by the holie Ghost, (Augustine in the 4. booke against Cresconius, Chapt. 8.) Petilian (though otherwise full of great bragging) being verie vnwilling to haue open disputation in any open assembly of learned men, vsed this arrogant speach: *Indignum est vt in vnum conueniant filij martyrum, & progenies traditorum.* It is an vnworthie thing that the sonnes of the Martyres and the generations of traitors should be assembled together. Thus much may suffice for this poynt. Where we see that the Donatists departed disorderlie out of the Church, condemning it not for any poynt of doctrine (for therein they did not disagree) but for that many, which in the time of persecution

secution dissembled, many which reuolted, and to saue their liues did sacrifice to the Idolls: many which deliuered the bookes of holie Scripture to bee burned, and betraied the names of the brethren; when the storme was ouer, & there was a sodaine calme, the Emperour Constantine being become Christian, such ioy in all Christian lands, Christianitie magnified with such honour: for that (I say) many such returned to professe the Gospell againe as members of the Church, and were receiued. For, saide the Donatists, the Church is holie, consisting of such as be called forth and separated from the vnpure and wicked world: and therefore no separation being made, but such villanous traitors, so vile Idolaters, and their childrē being communicated withall, all your assemblies through this mixture are none other before GOD, but heapes of abominable vncleane persons. Your teachers are the sonnes of Apostates and traitors, and no Ministers of Christ. Now looke vpon the Donatists of England: Antichrist hath béen exalted according to the prophesie of S. Paule, he hath sate in the Temple of God, boasting himselfe as God, persecuting and murthering Gods true worshippers. He is disclosed by the glorious light of the Gospell: his damnable doctrine, cursed Idolatrie, and vsurped tyrannie are cast forth of this land by the holie sacred power of our dread Soueraigne Ladie Quéene Elizabeth, whom God hath placed & settled vpon the Throne of this noble Kingdome. The true doctrine of faith is published, and penalties are by lawes appoynted for such as shall stubbernlie despise the same. Our Donatists crie out, that our assemblies, (as ye may see in their printed bookes) and that the people were all by constraint receiued immediatlie from Idolatrie into our Church without preaching of the Gospell, by the sound of a Trumpet at the Coronation of the Queene, that they bee confused assemblies, without any separation of the good from the bad. They affirme also that our Ministers haue their discent and ordination, and power, from Antichrist, and so are his marked seruants. Hereupon, not vnderstanding the manifest Scripture, that the Aposta-

sie hauing inuaded the Church, it continued still euen then
the Temple of God in which Antichrist did sit, and that the
verie Idolaters were within the Church, were sealed with
the signe of baptisme, professed Christ in some points rightlie, their children from ancient discent being within the couenant of God, and of right to bee baptized, the Ministerie of
Christ so farre remaining, as that it was the authentick seale
which was deliuered by the same; in a mad furie, like blind
hypocrites they condemne the reformation by ciuill power,
and purging Gods Temple by the authoritie of Princes,
because the Church of Christ is founded and built by the
doctrine of the Gospell. Herein they are deceiued, that they
imagine the Princes take vpon them to compell those to bee
a Church which were none before: whereas indeed they doo
but compell those within their kingdome ouer whome the
Lord hath set them, which haue receiued the signe of the couenant, and professe themselues to bee members of the
Church, accordinglie to renounce and forsake all false worship, and to imbrace the doctrine of saluation. What other
thing did Iosias and other holie Kings of Iuda, when they
compelled the multitude of Idolaters which were the seede
of Abraham, and circumcised, to forsake their Idolatrie and
to worship the Lord? It is most cleere also, that where the
reformation of the Kings was not perfect, (as appeareth in
the bookes of the Kings and Chronicles) yet all the foulest
things being abolished, and the substance of trueth brought
in, they were reputed godlie Churches, where many were
false brethren and open offenders. The Brownists blinded
with their swelling pride, and not seeing the euident matters
of the Scriptures, without all order of that holie discipline
of Christ, accuse, condemne and forsake our Churches, vnder the appearance of feruent zeale, and rigorous seueritie
against all sinne, not inferiour to the Donatists; as if they
were the onely men that stood for Christ and his kingdome,
they crie out aloude and proclaime all the Ministers of our
Churches to be Antichristian, the sonnes of the Pope, false
Prophets, Baals Priests, that prophesie in Baal, and pleade

for Baal, persecutors of the iust, bearing the marke, the power and life of the beast, because they say our ordeiners bee such. They say wee haue no word of God, no Sacraments nor true Church, but that all is vtterlie polluted and become abominable: our assemblies they call the very Synagogs of Antichrist, vtterlie fallen from the couenant of God, and all that ioyne with them, through the pollution of open sinners which are not cast forth: and therefore they haue separated themselues, and crie aloude vnto others to doo the same if they will be saued. What rule of discipline haue they obserued in this? Haue these things béen brought forth, scanned, discussed, and iudged in the Synods of the learned Pastors and teachers of the Churches? Nay, but euen as Augustine saith of the other, *furor, dolus, & tumultus*, furie, deceipt and tumult, do beare the sway. Then I conclude, that in this poynt of accusing, condemning, and manner of separating themselues from the Church, the Donatists and the Brownists doo agree and are alike. Some man will here replie, that I build vppon a weake ground, or rather vpon the sand, in prouing the Brownists and the Donatists to bée all one, because they are alike in accusing and condemning the Churches, and separating themselues from the same. For the matter resteth not simply vpon the actions; but whether there were iust cause. The question will bee whether the Brownists doo that iustlie, which the Donatists did vngodly. For the Donatists did accuse the Churches and Ministers fallsely, condemned them most wickedly, and therefore their separation could not bee good, because it was from the true Churches of Christ: but now if the Brownists obiect open and manifest crimes, such as cannot be denied, their case doth differ farre. May not a man separate himselfe from those assemblies, where he seeth open sinners suffered on heapes to remaine in the bosome of the Church, and where idolatries, blasphemies and abominations are committed, where the Ministers and gouernment be Antichristian, but he must bée a Donatist? Moreouer, it is certaine the Donatists did condemne all Churches in the world; the Brownists doo con-

demne onely the assemblies as they generally stand in England, which is a very great difference. The Donatists hold that the Sacraments or the efficacie of them doth depend vpon the worthines of the Minister: the Brownists are not of that mind. The Donatists did rebaptize; the Brownists doo vrge no such thing. It may be also they are vnlike in some other things: if it be so, why should they be termed Donatists? Indeed if there be such differences, the Brownists haue great wrong to bee called Donatists, and to bee condemned with so wicked a sect: But what if it fall out otherwise, and that it be shewed and proued manifestlie that they be all one in these things? Shall wee not then say they be euen brethren: shall they not stand or fall with the Donatists: shall they be vngodlie Schismatickes, and not these: I will procéede from poynt to poynt, to compare them together, that it may appeare whether there be difference. Touching the first, it is most true that the Donatists did accuse and condemne the Churches and the Ministers of the Churches most falselie: and I say the Brownists are as false accusers as they, and condemne as iniustlie in all crimes which they obiect, and shall in no wise bee found vnlike in this poynt. Yea, will it bee sayd, how shall that appeare: All men doo knowe that the Brownists may without any false accusing lay greeuous faults to the Church of England. I graunt they may: and I say likewise, the Donatists might lay as great faults to the charge of many Churches then, and in some points greater, & yet be no liers. This is to be proued by comparing the Churches of those times with ours: for so shall wee see how farre both haue iustlie accused, or might accuse, and where they meete together as false accusers. The Brownists may stand forth and accuse the church of England in this manner: That there bee heapes of open sinners not separated from among the good, but suffered and admitted to the Lords table, at least wise in many, or in the most assemblies: There be prophane ignorant persons that despise the holie religion: There bee swearers and cursers: There bee those that are puffed vp and swell in pride and
vaine

vaine glorie: There be swarmes of drunkards, gluttons and vnchast persons: There be couetous worldlings, and greedie vsurers, extortioners, oppressors, bribers and defrauders: There be liers, backbiters, and slanderers: There bee enuious, hateful and contentious persons: yea, what sinnes almost are wanting? Where shall a man goe but he is readie to fall into companies of wicked men? This is not alone among the common people; but verie many of those that should bee guiders, lights, and patternes of godlinesse vnto others, are nothing lesse. Who is able to deny these things? heauen and earth will witnesse against him. We may lift vp our voyces and say: wee haue sinned with our fathers, wee haue done wickedlie. We may confesse that our iniquities are heaped vp and reach aboue the clowdes, and that shame and confusion of face is due vnto vs. Wee may crie, saue Lord for the godlie cease, the faithfull are diminished from the children of men. The complaints that the Prophets doo make euerie where against the Church of Israel, may verie well be applied against vs. Where is loue, where is fidelitie, where is mercie, where is trueth? But now shall wee thinke that the Donatists had no such things to accuse the Churches of in those daies? Could they not say your assemblies are full of couetous men, proud persons both men and women? Had they not iust cause to complaine that many walked in hatred and discord? Doo ye imagine that there were no vngodlie Ministers? or will ye suppose that Augustine and other holie men stoode to cleere and iustifie the Churches that way against the Donatists and other Heretickes? Nay, let their words bee heard what they testifie in this behalfe. Cresconius alleaged this saying of the Lord, I will giue ye shepheards according to my heart, which shal feede yee with knowledge and vnderstanding. Ieremy. 3. This he cited to proue that the Pastors ought to bee faithfull. Augustine maketh answere thus: *Scio, completum est, tales Apostoli fuerunt, tales etiam nunc, etsi pro ecclesia latitudine perpauci, non tamen desunt.* That is, I knowe it is fulfilled, such were the Apostles, such also there be now, though very fewe in respect of the largenes of the Church, yet they are not wanting. This is a plain testimonie that in the time of Augustine the faithfull sincere godlie Pastors were verie fewe in comparison. Many testimonies may be brought out of diuers ancient writers for this matter: but I will bring but some fewe, and first out of Cyprian, which alone are sufficient being both large and cleere. Cyprian was in the time of persecution before the Donatists sprung vp; and after one persecution was ouer, he wrote an Epistle *de lapsis*, of those that fell and denied Christ: In which first he triumphantly reioyceth ouer them which stoode; then he mourneth dolefullie for those that fell: and after that he sheweth why God sent that persecution. *Si cladis causa cognoscitur, & medela vulneris inuenitur, Deus probare familiam suam voluit.* If (saith he) the cause of the slaughter be knowne, the cure of the wound is found also, God would prooue his familie. *Et quia traditam nobis diuinitus disciplinam pax longa corruperat, iacētem fidem, & pœnè dixerim dormientem, censura cœlestis erexit.* That is, and because long peace had corrupted the discipline deliuered vs of God, the heauenlie censure hath raised vp the faith lying along, I may say almost sleeping. Then shewing that God did not punish them so much as they deserued, he setteth forth the greeuous open sinnes committed in the Church. *Studebant augendo patrimonio singuli, & obliti quid credentes, aut sub Apostolis ante fecissent, aut postmodum facere deberent, insatiabili cupiditatis ardore ampliandis facultatibus incubabant.* That is, They studied euerie one to increase their patrimonie, and hauing forgotten either what the beleeuers had done before in the time of the Apostles, or what they ought to doo afterward, they all did applie themselues to increase their riches with an insatiable burning heate of couetous desire. Here is one sinne that ouerspread: then he addeth further. *Non in Sacerdotibus religio deuota, non in ministris fides integra, non in operibus misericordia, non in moribus disciplina.* There was not deuout religion in the Priests, there was not the sound faith in the Ministers, there was not mercie in workes, there was not discipline in manners. And what more? *Corrupta barba in viris, in fœminis forma fucata. Adulterati post dei manus oculi, capilli mendacio colorati. Ad decipienda corda simplicium callidæ fraudes, circumueniendis fratribus subdolæ voluptates. Iungere cum infidelibus vinculum matrimonij, prostituere cum gentilibus membra Christi. Non iurare tantum temerè, sed adhuc etiam peierare. Præpositos superbo tumore contemnere, venenato ore sibi maledicere. Odijs pertinacibus inuicem dissidere.* The beard was corrupted, or disguised, in men: the beautie was counterfeit or painted in women. The eyes corrupted from the forme in which Gods hands had made them, the haires were set out with a false colour: subtill fraudes to deceiue the hearts of the simple; deceiptfull pleasures to circumuent the brethren. They coupled themselues in mariage with infidels; they prostituted the members of Christ with the heathen: they did not onely sweare rashlie, but also forsweare. They contemned their gouernours with swelling pride, and cursed themselues with venymed mouth, being at discord among themselues with stiffe hatreds. Are not these horrible sinnes which ouerflowed in the church? Is there no more? Yes, he saith, *Episcopi plurimi, quos & ornamento esse oportet ceteris, & exemplo, diuina procuratione contempta, procuratores rerum secularium fieri, derelicta cathedra, plebe deserta, per alienas prouincias oberrantes negociationis quæstuosæ nundinas aucupari. Esurientibus in ecclesia fratribus habere argentum largiter velle, fundos insidiosis fraudibus rapere, vsuris multiplicantibus fœnus augere.* That is, very many Bishops, which ought to bee an ornament and an example vnto other men, despising the deuine cure, became factors in worldly matters, leauing the chaire, forsaking the people, wandring through other Prouinces, did hunt after faires or markets of gainefull trafficke. The brethren hungring in the Church they had siluer in great plentie: they would in rauening manner get lands by subtill fraud, increase their gaine with vsurie. What shall we say, did this holie Cyprian falselie accuse the Churches of his time, in laying these greeuous crimes

 to

to the charge both of the Pastors and the people: Doubtles he spake the trueth. It will be demaunded whether Cyprian and the rest of the godlie did worship together with those open sinners, ioyning with them in praier & receiuing the Sacraments. We see it is manifest they did: for he describeth not the heathen, or such as had been cast forth of the Church, but such as God sent chasticement vpon to raise vp the faith which was almost, as he saith, a sleepe. He doth also testifie in plaine wordes, that the godlie could not separate themselues from the Church, because of such open sinners, without proud obstinacie and sacrilegious presumption. He speaketh vpon this occasion: there were certaine which had suffered imprisonment for the Gospell; among whom was one Maximus an Elder, and certaine brethren, which when they came out of prison, separated themselues from the Church, taking offence at the open sinners which were not cast forth, as it appeareth by the words of Cyprian. For hauing testified his gladnes þ they had forsaken their schisme, and did returne againe into the Church: he addeth, *Nam etsi videntur in ecclesia esse zizania, non tamen impediri debet aut fides, aut charitas nostra, vt quoniam zizania esse in ecclesia semper cernimus, ipsi de ecclesia recedamus. Nobis tantummodo laborandum est, vt frumentum esse possimus, vt cum cœperit frumentum dominicis horreis condi, fructum pro opere nostro & labore capiamus.* That is, Although there bee tares seene to be in the Church, yet neither our faith nor our charitie ought to be hindered, that because wee alwaies perceiue tares to be in the Church, wee our selues should goe out of the Church: wee must onely labour that we may bee corne, that when the corne shall begin to be layd vp in the Lords barnes, wee may receiue fruit for our work & labour. Then further he addeth: *Apostolus in Epistola sua dicit, in domo autem magna, non solũ vasa sunt aurea, & argentea, sed & lignea, & fictilia, et quedã quidẽ honorata, quædã vero inhonorata: nos operã demus, & quantum possumus laboremus vt vas aureũ, vel argenteũ simus.* The Apostle in his Epistle saith, but in a great house there are not onely

onely vessels of gold and siluer, but also of wood and earth, and some vnto honour, and some vnto dishonour: let vs doo our endeuour, and labour what we can, that wee may be vessels of gold, or at least of siluer. Finallie he saith: *Caterum fictilia vasa confringere domino soli concessum est, cui & virga ferrea data est. Esse non potest maior domino suo seruus: nec quisquam sibi quod soli filio pater tribuit vendicarit, vt se putet vniuersa posse zizania, humano iudicio segregare: superba est ista obstinatio, & sacrilega presumptio, quam sibi furor prauus adsumit, & dum sibi semper quidam plus quam mitis iusticia deposcit, assumunt, de ecclesia pereunt: & dum se insolenter extollunt, ipso suo tumore cæcati, veritatis lumen amittunt.* But it is graunted onely to the Lord to breake the earthen vessels, to whom also the yron mace is giuen. The seruant cannot be greater than his Lord, neither shall any challenge that to himselfe, which the father hath giuen to the sonne alone, that he should think he can by humane iudgement seuer all the tares. That is a proud obstinacie and sacrilegious presumption, which wicked furie doth take to it selfe. And while some doo alwaies take more vpon them, than meeke iustice dooth require, they perish out of the Church: and while they insolentlie extoll themselues, being blinded with that very swelling of theirs, they lose the light of the trueth. What can be more manifest than these testimonies, which shewe that there were greeuous open sinnes committed by multitudes in the Church, not onely of the common sort, but euen of the teachers? We see they did communicate together, as in the old Church vnder the law, heapes of notorious wicked men did flock vnto the Temple and worship at the same Altar and Sacrifices with the godlie. Hierom in his Epistle to Paulinus sheweth, there were many of all sorts, both men and women, which did presumptuouslie, ignorantlie, & with vaine glorie prattle of the scriptures, and so abuse the holie word of God. And in the Ministrie there were that had stepped from seculer learning to deale with the Scriptures, which being able to rowle out words, thought they made goodlie sermons. Therefore if the

the Donatists had but complained that there were multi-tudes of open sinners in the Church, as proude, couetous, hatefull persons, irreligious and prophane abusers of the Scriptures, and not only of the common sort, but also of the teachers: their complaint had béen true. But when they proceeded thus; That all that did communicate with any such open sinners, were polluted by them, and fell from God: and so termed all the Pastors wicked traitors and Iudasses, wretches, whose worship and praiers were abominable, and all the people that ioyned with them prophane and heathen: therein they became false accusers and wicked condemners: they did with most intollerable pride and sacrilegious trea-cherie publish a diuorse betweene Christ and his spouse. The Brownists offend in the same degree in accusing, con-demning, and casting forth the Churches of Christ, affir-ming that by open sinners admitted to the Lords table, all are fallen from the couenant of grace, haue no true Sacra-ments, nor Church, but are as an heape of polluted heathen, whose worship and praiers are abominable.

Now that it may appeare vnto euery one that will not shut his eyes, that in this point our Brownists, (I speake of the Capitaines) are full Donatists, I wil enter into the par-ticular discourses, and shew vpon what Scriptures they stood, and with what arguments they maintained this their wicked hereticall opinion. And what answere they recea-ued from the holie seruants of God, the pastors of the Chur-ches. Wherein I desire the reader to obserue whether there may be found one haire breadth of difference between them: talke with the Brownists about this point which they hold, that where open sinners are admitted to the participation of the Sacraments, all which communicate with them are polluted, and cast away: or reade the bookes and writings of theirs which are spread, marke well the sentences and pla-ces of Scripture which they alleage and quote, and what reasons they drawe out of them, and then looke vpon these. For I will note the chiefe Testimonies of holy Scripture that the Donatists did alleage, to proue that all Churches
were

were polluted by the mixture of open sinners, and that a separation was commaunded by God from such assemblies, which are these. Come out from among them (saieth the Lord) and touch no vncleane thing, and I will receaue yee, and I will be your Father, and you shall be my Sonnes and my Daughters, saith the Lord God Almightie. 2.Cor.6. Haue no fellowship with the vnfruitefull workes of darkenes but rather reproove them. Ephes.5. Bee not partakers of other mens sinnes. 1.Tim.5. A little leauen dooth leauen the whole lumpe; and take away the euill from among yee. 1.Cor.5. If anie which is called a Brother be a Fornicator, an Idolater, or couetous, &c. with such see that yee eate not. 1.Cor.5. What hath the Chaffe to doo with the Corne? Ierem.23. Also depart, depart, come out from thence, and touch no vncleane thing, come out from the middest thereof and seperate your selues, yee that beare the vessels of the Lord. Isay.52. All these and some other did Parmenian the Donatist Bishop alleage in his Epistle. Wee may not thinke that these Scriptures were alleaged onely by some one Donatist: for Augustine in his booke *De vnico Baptismo* against Petilian Chapter 14. saith, *Magis enim solent in ore habere, quando peccatis aliorum alios criminantur, ad excusandum nefas separationis suæ, videbas furem & concurrebas cum eo, &c.* For they are wont rather to haue in their mouth, when they accuse some to be guiltie or polluted by the sinnes of other, to excuse their wicked seperation? Thou sawest a theefe and diddest run with him. Psal.50. And be not partakers of other mens sinnes, depart and come out from thence, touch no vncleane thing, & he that shal touch that which is vncleane shal be poluted, and a little leauen dooth leauen the whole lump, and other such like. Now what the estate of the question was, (and how they held men polluted, if they did not seperate themselues) the disputation betweene the Catholique Bishops and the Donatists which were assembled at the cōmaundement of the Emperour dooth shew. Where the names of the Donatist Bishops that had subscribed their consent to that confe-

 rence.

rence, were two hundreth seauentie and nine, but some of them were not there. Thus Augustine reporteth their words in the conference of the third day. Chapter 4. *Quia & in eo quod dicebant, & diuinis testimonijs velut astruebant, non esse malos in ecclesia tolerandos, sed ab eis recedendum propter contagium peccatorum: Ita se dicere demonstrabant, vt tamen ignoratis peccatis alienis neminem maculari posse faterentur.* Because euen in that which they saide, and which they did as it were confirme by the Scriptures, that the euil are not to be tolerate in the Church, but wee must depart from them for feare of the contagion of their sins: they shewed that they spake it to be vnderstoode thus, that neuerthelesse they confessed, that no man could be spotted with other mens sinnes which are secret. In this conference the Donatist Bishops stoode vpon this, that the Lord saith of the Church Esay. 52. There shall no vncircumcised or vncleane passe through thee anie more. And vpō that which is writtē by the Prophet Hag. chap. 2. Ask the Preests concerning the Lawe. If a man carrie holie flesh in the lappe of his garment, and the lappe of his garment shall touch the bread, &c. Shall he bee sanctified? The Priests answered, no. Then if a man that is vncleane touch any of those things, shall it not bee vncleane? The Priestes answer, it shall bee vncleane. So is this people, and so is this Nation before me saith the Lord, and so is the whole work of their hands, yea that which they haue offered there, hath been vncleane. Stay now and see whether the very same Scriptures bee not in the mouthes of the common sort of the Brownists, and whether the writings of the chiefe Brownists bee not euerie where spatred with the quotations of them. And to proue the same thing which the Donatists held, and maintained by them; namelie that such as communicate with open sinners are polluted by their sinnes, and therefore they separate themselues: But that this agreement betweene them may yet more fully appeare, I will proceed further and shewe how these matters were discussed. For otherwise it maye bee, some man will imagine that the

the auncient Fathers might defend the Churches against those allegations of the Donatists after such a sort as wee canne not truly defende ours at this day. Whereas therefore it was by the Donatists urged; depart, depart, come out from among them, seperate your selues, touch no uncleane thing, &c. the answere was by the Pastors of the Churches, that this seperation was not to bee made in bodie when the Church is pestered with open sinners, but in heart, and not consenting in minde unto the sins openly committed by those with whom they did communicate in the Church. These be the wordes of Augustine against Parmenian, in the second booke Chapt. 18. *Quæ verba isti carnaliter sentientes, per tot diuisiones seipsos minutatim in ipsa vna Aphrica conciderunt. Non enim intelligunt neminem coniungi cum infidelibus, nisi qui facit peccata Paganorum, vel talia facientibus fauet: Nec quenquam fieri participem iniquitatis, nisi qui iniqua vel agit vel approbat. Quis autem communicat tenebris, nisi qui per tenebras consentionis suæ, dimisso Christo sequitur* Belial? *quis ponit cum infidelibus partem suam, nisi qui eius infidelitatis fit particeps? Ita enim templum dei esse desinit, nec se aliter simulachris adiungit. Qui autem sunt templum dei viui, & in medio nationis tortuosæ ac peruersæ apparent sicut luminaria in mundo verbum vitæ habentes, nihil eos quod pro vnitate tolerant inficit, nec angustiantur. quia in illis habitat & deambulat deus; & exeunt de medio malorum, atque separãtur interim corde, ne forté cum id facere per seditionem Schismatis volũt, prius a bonis spiritualiter, quam a malis corporaliter separentur.* That is to say, which words they vndetstanding carnally; (for he had before repeated their allegation, Come out from among them and touch no uncleane thing) they haue cut themselues by morsels into so many diuisiõs in that one Aphrica: for they doe not vnderstand that no man is ioyned with Infidels, but he that doth commit the sinnes of the Pagans, or else doth fauour those that doe such things: neither that any man can be made partaker of the iniquitie, but he that eyther doth the wicked things, or else doth approoue them.

 And

And who hath felowship with darknes, but he that by the darknes of his consent forsaking Christ doth follow Belial? who putteth his part with infidels, but he which is partarker of that infidelitie? for that way he ceaseth to be the tẽple of God, neither otherwise dooth hee ioyne himselfe to Idols. And they which are the temple of the liuing God, and in the middest of a crooked and peruerse generation appeare as lights in the world, hauing the word of life; nothing doth infecte them which they tolerate for vnities sake, neither are they pent vp in anie straight, because God dooth dwell in them and walke in them. And they depart out of the middest of the euill, and in the meane while are seperate, at leastwise in heart, least perhaps while they would doo that by sedition & Schisme, they should rather be spirituallie separated from the good, than corporallie from the bad. Thus farre Augustine, for seperation in heart when it cannot be in bodie. Againe he saith, answering Parmenian to this sentence, bee not partaker of other mens sinnes, chap. 20. *Nos dicimus, quod qui non facit malum, nec facienti consentit, & facientem arguit, firmus atque integer inter iniquos tanquam frumentum inter paleas, conuersatur.* We say that he which dooth not commit euill, nor consent to him that dooth, and rebuketh him that dooth, he is conuersant firme and sound among the wicked, as the corne among the chaffe. Now whereas the Donatists did replie that the separation from the open sinners which God commandeth could not be meant of a separation onelie in heart and mind, for so we ought to be separate from the heathen: with whom yet it was lawfull to eate, for S. Paul willeth If an infidell bid thee to a feast goe, but if anie that is called a brother bee a fornicator an idolater or couetous, with such see that yee eate not: this must needes be understood of a bodelie separation, the Brownists pressing this Argument, also as the Donatists did, say we might eate common bread with infidels, yea at the same common table with such ungodlie Christians as Paul forbiddeth to eate with, and therefore the commandement of the Apostle they say is plaine, which

all

all men ought to obey, that if open sinners come to the holy table of the Lorde, wee ought not there to eate with them. But let vs see the answer of Augustine in the third booke against Parmenian Chap. 3. His wordes in deede are manie, but I will set them downe, because they be so full and pregnant to declare, wherein the controuersie lay betweene the Donatists and the Churches, and why the Donatists made separation. *In hac velut angustia quaestionis, non aliquid nouum aut insolitum dicam, sed quod sanitas obseruat ecclesiae, vt cum quisque fratrum, id est Christianorum intus in ecclesiae societate constitutorum, in aliquo tali peccato fuerit deprehensus, vt anathemate dignus habeatur, fiat hoc vbi periculum Schismatis nullum est, atque id cum ea dilectione, de qua ipse alibi praecipit dicens, vt inimicum eum non existimetis, sed corripite vt fratrem, non enim estis ad eradicandum, sed ad corrigendũ: quod si se non agnouerit, neque poenitendo correxerit, ipse foras exiet, & per propriam voluntatem ab ecclesiae vnitate dirimetur. Nam & ipse dominus cùm seruis volentibus Zizania colligere dixit, sinete vtraque crescere vsque ad messem: praemisit causam dicens, ne forte cum vultis colligere Zizanea eradicetis simul & triticum. Vbi satis ostendit, cum metus iste non subest, sed omnino de frumentorum certa stabilitate, certa securitas manet: id est quando ita cuiusque crimen notum est omnibus, & omnibus execrabile apparet, vt vel nullos prorsus, vel non tales habeat defensores, per quos possit schisma contingere: non dormiat seueritas disciplinae, in qua tantò est efficacior emendatio prauitatis, quantò diligentior confirmatio charitatis, tum autem hoc sine labe pacis & vnitatis, & sine lesione frumentorum fieri potest, cùm congregationis ecclesiae multitudo ab eo crimine quod anathematizatur aliena est. Tunc enim adiuuat praepositum potius corripientem, quam criminosum resistentem: tunc se ab eius coniunctione salubriter continet, vt nec cibum cum eo quisquam sumat, non rabie inimica, sed coertione fraterna. Tunc etiam ille & timore percutitur & pudore sanatur, cum ab vniuersa ecclesia se anathematizatum videns, sociam turbam cum qua in delicto suo gaudeat, & bonis insultet non potest inuenire.*

 That

That is to say, As it were in this straight of the question. I will not speake any thing that is new or vnwonted,
but that which the soundnes of the Church dooth obserue: that when anie of the Brethren, that is of the
Christians, which haue place within in the vnitie of the
Church, be taken in some such sinne, that hee may bee
accounted worthie to bee excommunicate; let it bee
done where there is no danger of a Schisme, and the
same with that loue, of which hee commaundeth elsewhere, saying, esteeme him not as an enemie, but ad-
monish him as a Brother, for yee are not to roote vp,
but to amend. If that hee shall not acknowledge himselfe, neither reforme himselfe by repentance, hee shall
depart out, and by his owne will shall bee cut from the
vnitie of the Church. For the Lord himselfe, when he
saide to the seruants, which would gather the tares,
suffer both to grow together, shewed a cause, saying, *least
peraduenture while yee goe about to roote vp the tares, ye pluck
vp also with them the wheate.* Where hee dooth plainelie
shew, that when there is no such feare, but there remaineth a full securitie of the vndoubted stabilitie of the
corne; that is when the crime of any one is so knowne
to all, and appeareth execrable vnto all, that either it
can haue no defenders at all, or else not such by whome
there may a Schisme fall out: let not the seueritie of
discipline sleepe, in which the curing of the disease is so
much more effectuall, as the confirmation of loue is
more diligent. Then also this may bee done without
any blot of peace and vnitie, and without hurting the
corne, when the multitude of the assemblie of the
Church is free from that crime, for which the excommunication is denounced. For then they rather helpe
the pastor that dooth chastice, than the guiltie offen-
dor which resisteth, then euerie man dooth healthfullie
abstaine from his fellowship, and not so much as eate
meate with him, not of an enemie like mad rage, but
of a brotherlie reprehension. Then hee also is stricken
with

with feare, and healed through shame, when seeing himselfe excommunicate of the whole Church, cannot finde a multitude to bee of his fellowship with which hee may reioyce in his sinne, and insult ouer the good. Thus farre Augustine, which yee see expoundeth that place of Paul, with such eate not, of those that be excommunicate iustlie by the Church, shewing that this excommunication cannot be executed when such a multitude doo sinne that it would breede a Schisme, if they should be all cast foorth and so pluck vp the wheate: seeing as he sheweth this censure is ordained as a remedie to heale, and not to pluck vp and destroy. This point peraduenture will seeme strange vnto many, that the seueritie of the discipline should cease as it were when it is a multitude that dooth offend: and least it may be thought not to be his meaning and as he speaketh, that which the soundnes of the Church did obserue, I will shew how he proceedeth further in his answer, *Neque enim potest esse salubris a multis correptio, nisi cum ille corripitur, qui non habet sociam multitudinem, cum verò idem morbus plurimos occupauerit nihil aliud bonis restat quam dolor & gemitus, vt per illud signum quod Ezechieli sancto reuelatur illa si euadere ab illorum vastatione mereantur.* For neither can that reprehension by manie (saith hee) bee for health, but when he is reprehended, which hath not the multitude his companion. But when the same sicknes hath taken hold of verie manie, there remaineth nothing else to the good, but sorrowe and bewailing, that through that signe which is reuealed vnto holie Ezechiel, they may deserue to escape vnhurt and free from the destruction of those wicked.

When Augustine hath vttered this, a little after he bringeth in Paule himselfe for example in his practise: for he willed them to excommunicate the incestuous person, and he that had willed not to eate bread with a brother so called that were a fornicator, doth not will them to cast them foorth, and not to eate bread with them whom he complaineth of: 2. Epistle 12. that had not repented for the vncleannes, and

fornication

fornication and wantonnes which they had committed: for these he saith were many: and therefore that S. Paule doth not threaten that whē he came he would cast them forth, but he would, as he saith, bewaile them. The like we see in those that denied the resurrection, he willed them not to cast these forth, least a schisme might growe thereupon. After this he addeth, *Et re vera si contagio peccandi multitudinem inuaserit, diuina disciplina seuera misericordia necessaria est: nam consilia separationis, & inania sunt & perniciosa atque sacrilega, quia & impia & superba fiunt, & plus perturbant infirmos bonos, quam corrigant animosos malos.* That is: And in verie deede if the contagion of sinning hath inuaded the multitude, the seuere mercie of diuine discipline is necessarie: for the counsell or enterprises of separation are both vaine and pernicious, yea sacrilegious, because they become both wicked and proude, and doo more trouble the good which are weake, than chastice the sturdie ones which are euill. What can bee more vehementlie thundred out against the Donatists than this? and yet the Brownists which are the same in their schisme, may not bee spoken sharply vnto. Then a little after Augustine doth as it were conclude in this poynt: *Misericorditer igitur corripiat homo quod potest: quod autem non potest patienter ferat, & cum dilectione gemat atque lugeat, donec aut ille desuper emendet & corrigat, aut vsque ad messem differat eradicare zizania, & paleam ventilare.* Let a man therefore with mercie correct that which he can: and that which he cannot, let him beare with patience, and with loue let him mourne and lament, vntill he from aboue doo either redresse and amend, or else differre vntill the haruest to roote out the tares, and to winnowe out the chaffe. Here he alleageth the example of that holie Martyr Cyprian which had béen Bishop of Carthage, who describing the multitude to bee so full of grosse sinnes, yea verie many of his fellow Bishops spotted with very foule crimes, yet he communicated with them, though not in their sinnes, which he did euermore reprehend, but in the Sacraments

and

and holie worship of God. Furthermore, answering to the sentence alleaged by the Donatist out of Ieremie, what hath the chaffe to doo with the corne? He saith among all things the Donatists in this did bewray their sacrilegious swelling pride. For though being demaunded they would confesse themselues to be sinners; yet in this they did not onely challenge to be the true Church alone, but also such as the holie Church shall be after the last winnowing. *Cui sacrilega praesumptioni & nephandae elationi, quid addi possit ignoro.* That is, To which sacrilegious presumption and cursed abominable swelling, I knowe not what can be added. Reade the bookes of Browne and the writings of other Brownists, and ye shall euer and anon finde great outcries, as they charge vs, against our wicked tollerating. If it were swelling pride in the Donatists that caused them to denie any tollerating, what is it in the Brownists? But to proceede yet further, in the third booke against Cresconius, Chapter 50. hee saith: *Haec omnia displicent bonis, & ea prohibent, & cohibent quantum possunt, quantum autem non possunt ferunt, & sicut dixi, pro pace laudabiliter tolerant, non ea laudabilia, sed damnabilia iudicantes: nec propter zizania segitem Christi, nec propter paleas aream Christi, nec propter vasa inhonorata domum magnam Christi, nec propter pisces malos retia Christi derelinquunt.* That is to say, Al these things displease the good, and they forbid them and restraine them as much as they can, and as much as they cannot restraine, they beare: and as I haue saide, they tolerate laudablie for peace sake, not iudging the thinges laudable but damnable: neither doo they forsake the corne of Christ for the tares, nor the floaer of Christ because of the chaffe, nor the great house of Christ because of the vessells for dishonour, nor the nettes of Christ for the euill fishes. I haue shewed alreadie, that the Donatist Bishops when they were by the commandement of the Emperour assembled in great number at Carthage, that there might bee a conference, declared this to bee their mind: when they affirme that the good are polluted and cast away by communicating with the bad, that it is when

Matth.13. Matth.3. 1.Timo.5. Matth.14.

the sinnes are manifest. Now I thinke it is not amisse to shewe somewhat of their disputation, that the things which I alleage touching their opinions, may not seeme to be from some fewe, which peraduenture might differ from others. Looke in the conference of the third day, Chapt. 4. The Bishops of the true Church to proue that there should be open wicked sinners in the Church mingled together with the good vnto the end of the world, alleaged first that the Church is called Christes flower where the corne and the chaffe are mixed together, but he hath his fanne, and will purge his flower, and gather the corne into his barne, and burne the chaffe with vnquenchable fire. Matth. 3. The Donatists at the first rashlie replie, that there was not the word flower expressed in the Scripture: but when they were conuinced manifestlie in that, then they say the chaffe did signifie the hypocrites and close sinners: as though the chaffe did so resemble the corne, that it could not be discerned. Then next was alleaged the parable of the good seede and the bad, and that the seruants were forbidden to plucke vp the tares, least they should in plucking vp the tares, plucke vp also together with them the wheate, but they are willed to let them grow together vnto the haruest. Matth. 13. Now because it is expresly said that the Tares appeared or shewed themselues and that the seruants did discerne them, so ẏ it cannot be taken alone of close sinners: The Donatists did flie vnto ẏ Cauil, that the field is not ẏ church, because he saith, the field is this world. And so they stood vpon this, that ẏ godly & open sinners are together in ẏ world, but not in the Church: For they did alleage many testimonies to shew that the world is taken for the wicked. It was replied by the Catholike Bishops, ẏ the world was somtimes put in good part, as whē it is said, God was in Christ reconciling the world to himselfe: And indeed, if it were not taken to be the Church, & that the good seede & the bad in the field, were together in the Church, howe shoulde the seruants haue a desire to pluck them vp? what had they to doe to meddle with such as were without? or why should there be danger in rooting them vp, least they should

should together roote vp the wheat? Then further when it was said that our sauiour compareth the kingdome of heauen vnto a Net cast into the sea, which gathereth together of all sorts both good bad and, which when it is ful men draw to land, & gather the good into vessells, & cast the bad away. Math. 13. The Donatists to this said that the euill fishes did signifie close hypocrites, and such sinners as could not be espied. *Victi euidentia veritatis malos in ecclesia vsq; ad finem seculi permixtos esse, confessi sunt: sed occultos eos esse dixerunt, quoniam sic a sacerdotibus ignorantur, quemadmodum pisces intra retia cum adhuc in mari sunt a piscatoribus non videntur.* That is, Being ouercome with euidence of truth, they confessed that the euill are mixed in the Church euē to the end of the world, but they said they are secret because they are vnknowen of the Pastors, euen as the fishes within the nettes, while they are yet in the Sea are not seene of the fishers. But if the Donatists had beene asked whether the fishes together in the Net doe not see one another, what would they say? Howe then are they secret, and not seene of the Pastors, who are also together with thē in the Net? For they did erre in taking the Pastors to bee the fishers that shall draw the Net to the shoare. For expounding it, our Sauiour saith: The Angells shall goe foorth, and seperate the euill from among the iust. The Angels then are they that draw the Net to the shoare. Were those vngodly sinners secret as fishes vnder the water which the Prophets complained of in olde time, and yet did not in bodie seperate themselues from them in the Temple: The like may be demanded touching the Pharisies and Saduces, and the multitude of common people in the Church, from whom our Sauiour did not seperate himselfe in bodie. But the Donatists were impudent in denying that the Prophets and the other godly did worship together in the temple, and at the same Altare with the wicked multitude whom they so sharply reprehended.

Now may the reader see what the Donatists maintained, and wherefore they seperated themselues: which I will expresse in the wordes of Augustine in his third booke against Cresconius Chapt. 81. *Ibi enim tota defensio vestra consistit, quia propterea vos separastis, ne aliorum peccatorum contagione periretis: vnde nouum genus area vos fecisse gloriamini, aut qua solum triticum habeat, aut in qua solum triticum appareat, cui non sit necessarius ventilator, sed perscrutator.* That is For therein doth your whole defence consist, that therefore ye haue separate your selues, that ye might not perish by the contagion of other mens sinnes: wherevpon ye glorie that ye haue made a new kinde of floare, which either hath in it only wheat, or else in which there appeareth wheat alone which needeth not a winnower, but a searcher. The Donatists alleaging against the Churches for the open sinners mixed among them ye saying of Esay, wo be to thē that cal euill good and good euill, light darkenes, and darkenes light, &c. Augustine answereth, *Quisquis ergo vel quod potest arguendo corrigit, vel quod corrigere non potest, saluo pacis vinculo excludit, vel quod saluo pacis vinculo excludere non potest, aequitate improbat, firmitate supportat, hic est pacificus & ab isto maledicto immunis quod scriptura dicit, vae his qui dicunt quod nequam est bonum, &c,* Whosoeuer therefore dooth either amend that which hee can by reprouing, or that which he cannot amend, he casteth forth, the band of peace being kept safe, or that which he cannot cast out with rhe safetie of the band of peace, by equitie hee disaloweth, and beareth it with constancie: this man is the peacemaker, and is free from that curse which the Scripture pronounceth, *Woe be to them which cal euill good, &c.* Against Parmenian booke 2. chap. 1. The Donatists alleaging the sentences of the Prophets to proue that all ought to separate themselues from those, among whome the open notorious wicked men were suffered, and not cast forth: he answereth that they cited the testimonies of Scripture, and did not looke vpon the deeds of the Prophets, and so to know how the words of the Prophets were to be vnderstand. Then hee demaundeth, *Dixit Ieremias quid paleis ad triticum? Ut ipse recederet a paleis populi sui, in*

quas

quas illa tanta & vera dicebat? Did Ieremie ſay *What hath the chaffe to doo with the corne*, for this end, that he himſelfe ſhould depart from the chaffe of his people, againſt which hee did vtter thoſe ſo great things, and the ſame moſt true? *Dixit Ieſaias, Recedite, recedite, exite inde, & immundum nolite tangere. Sed cur ipſe in illo populo immunditiam quam grauiter arguebat, in vna cum eis congregatione tangebat? Legant quanta in malos populi ſui, & quam vehementer ac veraciter dixerit, a quibus ſe tamen nulla corporali diremptione ſeparauerit.* That is, Eſay ſaide, *Depart, depart, come out from thence, and touch not that which is vncleane.* But whie did hee himſelfe in one congregation with them, touch that vncleannes which hee reprooued in that people? They may read how great things hee vttered againſt the wicked of his people, how vehementlie and trulie, from whome notwithſtanding hee did ſeparate himſelfe with no bodelie ſeparation. After he hath ſhwed the like in the holie Prophet Dauid who profeſſed hee had not ſit in the counſell of vaine men, and yet was not ſeparate in bodie from the vngodlie in his dayes: He addeth *Nonne, ſi eorum verba factis eorum obijceremus reſponderent nobis, nos planè cum talibus nullum habuimus in corde conſortium, nec tangebamus immundum vbi poteſt coinquinari contactus: id eſt conſenſione atque placito conſcientiæ recedebamus, & exibamus ab eis, qui non ſolùm talia non faciebamus, ſed nec facientibus tacebamus.* If we ſhould obiect their words againſt their deedes, would they not anſwer vs, wee haue had vtterlie no fellowſhip in heart with ſuch wicked men, neither did we touch that which is vncleane, where the touching may be defiled: That is to ſay, wee did depart and come out from them in conſent and likening of conſcience, which our ſelues, not onelie, did not doo ſuch things, but alſo kept not ſilence to them that did ſuch wickednes. Againſt Parmenian booke 3. chap. 4. Again, in the ſame place he addeth, *Poſtremò ſi Prophetæ poſteros monuerunt vt ſe ante tempus vltimæ ventilationis a paleis corporaliter ſepararent, & taliſepa-*

 rationa

ratione cauerent tangere immundum, & cum facinorosis non introirent, cur hoc non fecit Apostolus Paulus? An palea nõ erant, qui non ex veritate, sed ex inuidia Christum annunciabant? An immundi non erant, qui non castè euangelium prædicarunt? Hos in illis temporibus ecclesia fuisse testatur, cuius excellentissimam charitatem omnia tolerantem, etiam posteriores imitati sunt. That is, Lastlie if the Prophets gaue warning to the posteritie that they should before the time of the last winnowing separate themselues from the chaffe in bodie, and by such separation take heede of touching any vncleane thing, and that way not to enter with the wicked dooers, whie did not the Apostle Paul doo so? Were not they chaffe which preached Christ of enuie, and not for the trueth? Were not they vncleane, which preached the Gospell not purelie? That there were such in the Church at those times hee dooth testifie Philip. 1. Whose most excellent charitie induring or tolerating all things, those that suceeded haue also imitated. Hauing thus affirmed, that this most excellent loue of Paul tolerating open wicked men in the church where they could not without danger of schisme be cast foorth was imitated of the godlie pastors that succeeded: he alleageth for example holie Cyprian: who testifying that not onelie the people, but also manie of his fellowe Bishoppes were horriblie wicked, yet liued in peace with them, and did not separate himselfe in bodie. Thus hee demaundeth, *An immunditia, an etiam auaritia, quam Cyprianus corde non tetigit, & tamen inter auaros collegas pacatissimè vixit?* Was it not vncleannes, was it not also couetousnes, which Cyprian touched not in heart, and yet liued most peaceablie among his couetous fellowe Bishops? He knew right well what God commaundeth in the Psalme, that hee should not sit in the counsell of vaine men, nor enter with the wicked dooers. *An non erat conuenticulum vanitatis in eis, qui esurientibus in ecclesia fratribus, largissimo argento nitere cupiebant? An non erant facinorosi qui fundos insidiosè fratribus rapiebant? An*

nequissimi

nequissimi & impij non erant qui vsuris multiplicantibus fœnus augebant? Ille vero, lauabat manus suas cum innocentibus & circundabat altare domini. Ideo quippe tolerabat nocentes, ne desereret innocentes cum quibus manus lauabat, quia diligebat speciem domus domini, quæ species in vasis honorabilibus fuit. That is, Was not the conuenticle of vanitie among them, which while their brethren indured hunger or penurie in the Church, did couet to shine gorgeouslie with most aboundant wealth? Were not they wicked dooers, which by deceiptfull meanes in such rauening sort tooke from their brethren possessions of Lands? Were they not most vngodlie and wicked, which with multiplying vsurie did increase their gaine? But Cyprian did wash his hands with innocents, and compassed the Altar of the Lord. He tolerated the wicked, least he should forsake those innocent, with whom hee washed his hands, because hee loued the beautie of the Lords house, which beautie was in the vessels for honour. Now where the Donatists might obiect, shall the discipline then be neglected, and wicked men suffered to liue at their pleasure in the Church? Augustine answereth both them and all others touching this obiection, first in his third booke against Parmenian chap. 1. *Quapropter quisquis etiam contempserit ecclesiæ Dei disciplinam vt malos cum quibus non peccat, & quibus non fauet, desistat monere, corrigere, arguere: si etiam talem gerit personam, & pax ecclesiæ patitur, vt etiam à sacramentorum participatione quempiam possit separare, non alieno malo peccat sed suo, ipsa quippe in tanta re negligentia graue malum est, & ideò sicut Apostolus admonet, si auferret malū a seipso, non solum auferret audaciam committendi, aut pestilentiam consentiendi, sed etiam pigritiam corrigendi, & negligentiam vindicandi abhibita prudentia & obedientia in eo quod præcepit dominus, ne frumenta lædantur.* That is to say, Wherfore, whosoeuer also shall despise the discipline of Gods Church, so that he giue ouer admonishing, correcting, and reprouing the euill men with whome hee dooth not sinne, and whome

whome he dooth not fauour, yea if he beare such office, and the peace of the Church permit, that hee may also separate any from the participation of the Sacraments, and dooth not, he sinneth by his owne falt and not by the falt of another. For the verie negligence it selfe in so great a matter is a grieuous sinne, and therefore as the Apostle dooth warne. If he will take away euil from himselfe, hee must not onelie take away the boldnes of committing it, or the pestilence of consenting thereto, but also the slouthfulnes of correcting and negligence of reuenging the same, prudentlie obeying in that which the Lorde hath commaunded, that the wheate may not be hurt.

In his third booke against Petilian, Chapt. 4. hauing before shewed that there is a worthie patience in suffering the false brethren for the vnities sake: he addeth, *Neque hoc ideo dixerim vt negligatur ecclesiastica disciplina, & permittatur quisque facere quod velit sine vlla correptione & quadam medicinali vindicta, & terribili lenitate, & charitatis seueritate.* That is, Neither haue I therefore sayd this, that the ecclesiasticall discipline should be neglected, and that euery one should be suffered to do what he will without rebuke, and without a certaine medicinable reuenge, terrible lenittie, and seueritie of loue. In the 37. Chap. of the same booke, hauing spoken of the corne and the chaffe mixed together, the wheate and the tares growing together, the good fishes and the bad in the same nette together vnto the end of the world, he then inferreth: *Nec propterea tamen ecclesiastica disciplina negligitur à constantibus, & diligentibus, & prudentibus dispensatoribus Christi, vbi crimina ita manifestantur, vt nulla possint probabili ratione defendi.* That is, Notwithstanding the ecclesiasticall discipline is not therefore neglected of the constant, diligent and wise dispensers of Christ, where the crimes are manifested in such sort that they can in no probable maner be defended. In the fourth Chapter of his booke after the conference with the Donatists, taking aduantage of a saying which they vttered, which was

was this: *Nec causa causa praeiudicat, nec persona persona.* That is, neither doth cause preiudicate cause, neither one person another. Hee saith that the cause and person of the tares doth not preiudicate the cause and person of the wheat growing together in the same field untill the haruest come: The cause and person of the chaffe doth not preiudicate the cause and person of the corne, beeing together in the same floare untill the last winnowing: The cause and person of the goates, doth not preiudicate the cause and person of the sheepe, kept together in the same pastures, untill the great shepheard shall separate them to the right hand and to the left in the last day: The cause and person of the euill fishes doth not preiudicate the cause and person of the good fishes, though they bee held in the same nette to be separated in the last shoare. Then he addeth, *Quibus parabolis, & figuris ecclesia praenunciata est vsque in finem seculi bonos & malos simul habitura, ita vt nec mali bonis obesse possint, cum vel ignorantur, vel pro pace & tranquillitate ecclesia tolerantur, si eos prodi aut accusari non oportuerit, aut alijs bonis non potuerit demonstrari: ita sanè vt nec emendationis vigilantia quiescat, corripiendo, degradando, excommunicando, caeterisque coertionibus licitis atque concessis, quae salua vnitatis pace in ecclesia quotidie fiunt secundum praeceptum Apostolicum charitate seruata qui dixit, si quis autem non obaudit verbo nostro, per epistolam hunc notate, & nolite commisceri cum eo, vt erubescat, & non vt inimicum existimetis, sed corripite vt fratrem. Sic enim & disciplina seruat patientiam, & patientia temperat disciplinam, & vtrumque refertur ad charitatem, ne forte aut indisciplinata patientia foueat iniquitatem, aut impatiens disciplina dissipet vnitatem.* That is to say, By which parables and figures, the Church is foreshewed that it shall haue the good and the bad together vnto the ende of the world, so as the euil cannot hurt the good, when either they are not knowne, or else are tolerated for the peace and tranquilitie of the Church, if it be not behoueful that they shal be manifested or accused, or that it cannot be shewed to others that be good: euen so verelie as yet the watchfulnesse

 of

of redresſing may in no wiſe reſt, in rebuking, degrading, excommunicating, and in other lawfull and allowable reſtraints, which, the peace of vnitie receiuing no dammage, are daylie practiſed in the Church without any hindrance or breach of loue, according to the Apoſtles precept, which ſayd: *If any obey not our word, note him by an Epiſtle, and haue no fellowſhip with him, that he may bee aſhamed, and eſteeme him not as an enemie, but admoniſh him as a brother.* For in ſo doing, the diſcipline doth keepe patience, and patience doth temper the diſcipline, and both are referred vnto charitie, leaſt either vndiſciplined patience ſhould foſter iniquitie, or impatient diſcipline, might diſſolue and ſcatter the vnitie.

Thus farre Auguſtine: by which words he ſheweth, that albeit the good and the bad ſhall alwaies euen to the end of the world bee mixed together on heapes in the Church, ſo that oftentimes open ſinners cannot bee all caſt forth without daunger of ſchiſme, and therefore are to be tollerated for the peace of the Church: yet the diſcipline is not to ſleepe, but ſinners are to bee rebuked: ſuch as beare publike office, if they deſerue, are to be degraded and depriued. The notorious wicked are to bee excommunicated, where the multitude is not guiltie with them, but that they may be forſaken of all and ſo made aſhamed: but loue, according to the rule of Saint Paule, is to ſit at the ſtearne and to order the whole matter, leaſt the ſeueritie of chaſticing diſcipline, if it were not mixed and tempered, or as I may ſay, delaied with patience, might breed tumults and ſchiſmes, and ſeparations: or leaſt on the other ſide, if tollerating patience were not ſharpened by the ſeueritie of diſcipline, it might nouriſh all manner of wickednes.

We ſee then what was the practiſe of the auncient Churches, and that touching the Eccleſiaſticall cenſures, the mixture of patience and ſeueritie, whollie referred vnto loue, doo make a ſoueraigne plaiſter and medicine, to ſalue and cure the ſores of the Church. Where theſe be not tempered together there is great decay: for as the rigorous ſeueritie of

Dona-

Donatisme, without any aswaging the heate of seueritie with the mixture of loue and patient colleration, doth rend vp and furiouslie teare all in peeces: so doth ouermuch or a loose sufferance (for it deserueth not the name of patience, not regarding Gods honor nor mens saluation) suffer the Lords field to ouergrowe with tares, and fill the Lords Courts with Goates and Swine: whereby holie things are greatlie prophaned, the weake are made to stumble, and many are cast downe. Touching this first point then in controuersie betwéene the Donatists and the Churches, I will conclude it with that which Augustine writeth in his treatise *De vnitate Ecclesiæ*, Chapt. 16. where hauing shewed in the former parts of the same booke that the controuersie was not about the head, which is Christ, but about the bodie, which is his Church. For touching the head they agreed, and touching the bookes of holie Scripture and their authoritie, there was no dissent at all betweene the Donatists and them.

Then further he commeth to this poynt, that as Christ the head is to bee sought for and knowne onlie in the Canonicall Scriptures: so the Church, which is his bodie, is likewise to be sought for, found out, and iudged onely by the same bookes of Scripture. Then he calleth for triall not by those darke places of the Byble which are spoken in figures and may be expounded diuers waies in probable sense; but from the manifest cléere testimonies, which also he alleageth out of many bookes both of the old and newe Testament, to proue that the Church should bee spread ouer all the kingdomes and nations of the world. He answereth the places of Scriptures which they alleaged to proue that the world at sundrie times had so fallen away from God, that a verie fewe true worshippers remained, and why might not they be now as those fewe? He sheweth that there be innumerable testimonies to proue, that the open bad did communicate together with the good in the Sacraments, and that the good were fewe in comparison of the bad so mixed with them, of which (after he hath cited many) he commeth at the last as it were to a conclusion, that al other things remoued, hee would haue them shewe their Church out of the holie Scriptures, and from the places which are not darke. And then it followeth, *Quisquis ergo huic epistolæ respondere se præparat, ante denunciationem mihi dicat, illi codices dominicos ignibus tradiderunt, illi simulacris gentium sacrificauerũt, illi nobis iniquissimam persecutionem fecerunt, et vos eis in omnibus consensistis. Breuiter enim respondeo quod sæpè respondi, aut falsa dicitis, aut si vera sunt, non ad frumenta Christi, sed ad eorum paleam pertinent ista quæ dicitis, non inde perit ecclesia, quæ optimo iudicio ventilata, istorum omnium separatione purgabitur.* That is to say, Whosoeuer therefore prepareth himselfe to answere this Epistle, let him before the denouncing, say vnto me; such deliuered the Lords bookes to the fire, such sacrificed to the Idols of the Gentiles, such haue persecuted vs most vniustlie, and you haue consented vnto them in all things. For I answer brieflie, which I haue often answered, either ye speake things which are false, or else if they bee true, that which ye speake pertaineth not to the corne of Christ but to the chaffe thereof, the Church doth not perish thereby, which winnowed with most perfect iudgement, shall bee purged by the separation of that same chaffe. He addeth: *Ego ipsam ecclesiã requiro vbi sit, quæ audiendo verba Christi & faciendo ædificat super petram, & audiendo & faciendo tolerat eos, qui audiendo & non faciendo ædificant super arenam. Vbi sit triticum quod inter zizania crescit vsque ad messem, non quid fecerint vel faciant ipsa zizania. Vbi sit proxima Christi in medio filiarum malarum, sicut lilium in medio spinarum non quid fecerint, vel faciunt ipsæ spinæ. Vbi sunt pisces boni qui donec ad littus perueniant, tolerant pisces malos pariter irretitos, non quid fecerint aut faciant ipsi pisces mali.* That is to say, I seeke the Church, where she is, which in hearing the words of Christ and doing them doth build vpon a rocke, and which hearing and doing doth tolerate those, which hearing and not dooing doo build vppon the sand. Where that wheate is which groweth vp among the tares vntill the haruest come, not

what

what the tares haue done, or what they doo. Where that ſpouſe of Chriſt is in the middeſt of the euill daughters, as the lillie among the thornes, not what the thornes haue done, or what they doo. Where the good fiſhes be, which vntill they come vnto the ſhore doo tolerate the euill fiſhes held in the ſame nette together, not what the euill fiſhes haue done, or what they doo.

Thus haue I laide open, that the Church in olde time was full of open wicked men both of miniſters and people: That the Donatiſts vnder the colour of zeale and ſeueritie againſt ſinne did ſeparate themſelues, affirming that all were polluted and fallen from the couenant, which did communicate in the worſhip of god and Sacraments with ſuch notorious euill men. All men may ſee by that which I haue noted, that the Donatiſts did maintaine this their opinion with the ſame Scriptures and argumẽts that the Browniſts doe maintaine it withall nowe: And receiued the ſame anſwers to confute them, which we make nowe to confute the Browniſts. This was the maine point of Donatiſme, and as it were the pith & ſubſtance therof: & it is one of the foure chiefe pillers of Browniſme. Yea but now the Browniſts doe ſeparate themſelues from a worſhip which is Idolatrous, full of blaſphemies and abhominations: The Donatiſts did rend themſelues from an holy and true worſhip. Indeede where the worſhip is Idolatrous and blaſphemous, a man is to ſeparate himſelfe. But there are many and great corruptions before it come to that: for it is the true worſhip of God where the foundation is layd and ſtandeth ſure. If there be timber, hay, and ſtubble built vpon the foundation, the fault is great, ſuch things are not to bee approued: But yet there is Gods true worſhip. And now to come to the verie poynt of the matter: I doe affirme & will ſtand to iuſtifie, that there were greater corruptions in the worſhip of God, euen in thoſe Churches from which the Donatiſts did ſeperate themſelues, than be at this day in the worſhip of the Church of England. So that if Browniſme be any thing to be excuſed in that, the Donatiſme may as iuſtly therein be defended. For if wee consider matters which concerne doctrine, what can any man shew so corrupt in this our Church, as in the publike worship to pray for the soules of the dead, and to offer oblations for the dead? This corruption was generall in the Church then, yea long before the dayes of Augustine, as it appeareth in Cyprian and by Tertullian which was before him, and nerer to the time of the Apostles; who in his booke De Monogamia reasoning against second mariage (for hee was fallen into that error) woulde perswade any woman that had buried her husband not to marie againe, because, he being seperated from her in peace & not diuorced, she was to pray for his soule, and yearely to offer oblation for him: thus he writeth, *Et pro anima eius oret, & refrigerium interim ad postulet ei, & in prima resurrectione consortium: & offerat annuis diebus dormitionis eius*. That is, And let her pray for his soule, and craue refreshing for him nowe in the meane time, and his felowship in the first resurrection, and let her offer yearely vpon the day of his departure. It will bee said by some ignorant man, that this was but the minde and practise of some few, which were corrupt and superstitious. I answere it was the practise of the Church in generall, and the corruption so auncient, that the same Tertullian in his booke *De corona militis*, speaking of it & certain other things saith they were obserued by tradition from the Apostles, they were obserued so generally in the Churches and no scripture to warrant them. These bee his wordes, *Oblationes pro defunctis, annua die facimus*. Wee make oblations for the dead in the yeerely day. The doctrine of Purgatory, and the doctrine of Free will were crept in also, besides diuers other grosse errors which sundrie of the chiefe teachers held, some in one poynt some in an other. Touching Ceremonies not for order and comlynes, but with signification, the libertie was exceeding which men tooke, and the corruption greeuous, which was not espied but of few. Tertullian for his time nameth these, which he saith were receiued by tradition and had no scripture to warrrant them. first in baptisme hauing shewed what they professed, and the three times

times dipping into the water, hee addeth. *Inde suscepti lactis & mellis concordiam pregustamus. Exque ea die lauacro quotidiano per totam hebdomadam abstinemus.* That is Taken from thence (hee meaneth from the water wee first taste the concord of milke and hony, and from that day we abstaine from the dayly washing a whole weeke. *Die dominico ieiunium nefas ducimus, vel de geniculis adorare: Eadem immunitate a die pascha in Penticostem vsque gaudemus.* That is, We account it an heynous matter to fast on the Lords day, or to worship vpon the knees: by the same freedome, from Easter vnto Penticost we reioyce. And by and by after hee saith. *Ad omnem progressum atque promotum, ad omnem aditum, & exitũ, ad vestitũ, ad calciamentũ, ad lauacra, ad mẽsas, ad lumina, ad cubilia, ad sedilia, quacunque nos conuersatio exercet, frontem crucis signaculo terimus.* That is, At euerie setting forward and mouing, at euerie comming to, or going foorth, at our appareling, and putting on our shooes, at washing at table, at lighting the candle, at bed, at sitting, whatsoeuer wee are busied about, we weare our forehead with the signe of the Crosse. These superstitious obseruations were crept into the Church, and in the daies of Tertullian who liued not much more than two hundreth yeares after our Sauiour Christ, receaued so generallie, that hee saieth they were by tradition from the Apostles. Augustine vnto Ianuarius complaineth that there was such a multitude of rites or ceremonies in the Church. But what should I labour in this point? If the Brownists will affirme that there be as great corruptions in the worship of the Church of England, if we respect either doctrine or ceremonies, as were in the Churches from which the Donatists did separate themselues, they shall be conuinced of grosse ignorance. And if they stand in it, they shall shew themselues shameles: let the reader in the meane time but looke vpon the Epistle of Master Beza before the new Testament, and see what he affirmeth in this matter, how corrupt the Churches were. Then I conclude that the Donatists separating themselues from Churches more corrupt than the Churche of England

England in the worship of God, as I dare stand to maintaine against them: if they denie it, may as well bee excused as the Brownists, and so hetherto they bee euen bretheren with them, or their naturall Children, no difference to bee found at all. And now touching the third and fourth pillars of Brownisme; the Donatists cried out that the Churches had no true Ministers, but that they were all false Prophets, Iudasses, persecutors of the iust, generations of Traitors, because as they saide they had their ordination from those that were such. The Brownists with all their might lift vp their voices, and call vs Baals Priests, the marked seruants of Antichrist, false Prophets, seducers and such like, because, as they say, we are ordeined by Antichristian Bishops, which exercise a Discipline contrarie to the Discipline of Christ. Here wee haue to consider of two things at once the Ministers and the Discipline: let vs first see what the Donatists held against the Ministers. This was the common voice among the Donatists, O that matters might be disputed, discussed, and scanned. But when by the commandement of the Emperour, the conference should bee holden what miserable shiftes and delayes did they finde out? And in the conference of the third day, Chapt. 2. It is shewed that the Donatists did accuse them as Traitors and persecutors: and that this saying had been vttered. *Indignum est vt in vnum conueniant filij Martyrum & progenies traditorum.* It is an vnworthie thing, that the sonnes of Martyres, & the generations of traitors should come together. When Augustine had saide he was no traitor, Cresconius the Donatist replieth. *Sed ille qui tradidit te, creauit. Fonte deducitur riuus, & caput membra sequuntur, sano capite omne sanum est corpus, & si quid in hoc morbi vel vitij est, omnia membra debilitat, or iginem suam respicit quicquid in stirpe processit. Non potest innocens esse qui sectam non sequitur innocentis.* But he that created thee plaied the Traitor, the riuer or streame is deriued from the Fountaine, and the members followe the head. The head being sounde, the whole bodie is found, and if there bee anie disease in it, it

weakeneth

weakeneth all the members. It respecteth it owne originall, whatsoeuer groweth out of the stock: hee cannot bee innocent, which followeth not the sect of the innocent. These be the words of Cresconius the Donatist, by which hee taketh vpon him to proue that Augustine, and all the Pastors of the Churches had no true ordination, were not true Ministers of Christ, but the generations of traitors: He vseth as we see thrée similitudes. The first is to this effect, as the riuer is deriued from the Fountaine, and must néedes be such as it is, so those that bée ordeined Ministers are like the streame deriued from the fountaine, the ordeinors being traitors, Judasses, false prophets, persecutors; ÿ ordeined must néedes be such also. The second is that the members doo followe the head: He that ordeineth is the head, the Ministers ordeined are the members. If the head be infected, the poyson of it goeth into the mẽbers, Thy ordeinor, euen thy head was a traitor, thou art then a traitor also. The third similitude is from the stock and the branches that growe out of it: such as the stock is, such are the braunches that growe out of it. But he that ordeined thée or created thée a Minister, was a false Prophet: therefore thou art a false prophet: for hée is the stock out of which thou doost growe, how canst thou but bee such as the roote, out of which thou doost spring. The Brownists handling this point, to proue that we be no Ministers of Christ set foorth the matter thus: your discent and pedegrée is in few degrées deriued from the Pope, you being the Children of your Antichristian Bishops, which are the creatures of the Pope, who is the eldest sonne of Sathan, and his vicar generall in earth, whose image, marke, power, and life you beare, and together with him growe, liue, raigne, stand, and fall as the branches with the Trée. This is the eloquence of the Brownists, which differing in words, containeth the same reasons that the Donatists did vse: for in stead of the Fountaine and the streame, the head and the members, they put the Fathers and the Children: for the stock and the braunches they put the Trée and the boughes which is all one: And from the roote, as it were from the Fountaine and head, they deriue the life, the power and the Image, &c. Thus they agrée then, that the one part saide those which ordeined ye were such as sacrificed to Idols, and Traitors, verie Iudasses, you are their children and like them. The other part saieth, those that ordeined yee bée the creatures of Antichrist, yée receiue the verie life and power of your Ministerie from them, ye are their Children, and so the Children of the Pope. Now let vs sée the answer which Augustine maketh, which is this, *In his omnibus verbis tuis creatorem meum caput meum, non fecisti nisi traditorem, quem quidem accusare tantùm, non conuincere potuisti. Ego autem nec eius innocentiam mihi creatricem vel fontem caputúe constituo. Sed tu ad illud redis in quo Petilianus errauit, cum cuiusq; in sanctificatione baptismatis Christus sit origo caputq; nascentis: & nos vis venire in maledictũ, de quo scriptum est: maledictus omnis qui spem suam ponit in homine.* That is to say, In all these thy wordes thou hast made my ordainer, my head, none other than a traitor, whom thou couldest onely accuse, but not conuince. But I do not hold his innocencie to be that which hath ordained me a Minister, or to be fountaine or head: but thou doest returne to that in which Petilian erred, when as Christ in the sanctification of baptisme is the originall and the head of euerie one that is borne againe: and wilt haue vs come into the curse, of which it is written: *Cursed is euerie one that putteth his trust in man.*

Thus farre Augustine, whose answere hath two parts. The first is, that the Donatists did accuse, but could not proue that the ordainers were such as in time of persecution had yeelded to sacrifice to Idols, or deliuered the holie booke to the fire. The other part is, that whether he that ordained him were a godlie man or a wicked man: the matter is all one touching his ordination and Ministrie. The ordination not being mans, the innocencie of man cannot be the ordainer, it cannot bee the head or fountaine: neither can it make his ordination the better. Then likewise, the wickednesse of the man that ordaineth, cannot be the roote nor the fountain,

nor

nor the head. The men which ordaine, are not the fathers of the Ministrie, because it is not theirs which they deliuer, but Christs. That this is Augustines meaning it is cléere by that he telleth Cresconius he returned to that in which Petilian erred. Petilian denying that it was baptisme that had béen ministred by an vngodlie man: rendereth this reason, that euerie thing must haue an originall and an head, or else it is nothing. Augustine replieth, that Christ onely is the originall and the head of him that is baptized: and that the baptisme being Christs, and not theirs that did deliuer it: the goodnes of the Minister made it not one iot the better, nor the wickednes of the Minister any whit the worse. Adding moreouer, that such as take the baptisme ministred by a godlie man to bee better in it selfe, than that which is ministred by a naughtie man: fall into the curse, of which it is written, Cursed is euerie one that putteth his trust in man. He that hangeth the matters which are Christs vpon men, putteth his trust in men. The same answere that hée hath made to those his Donatists of Aphrica, doo wee make vnto our Donatists of England. First they accuse in most bitter and hainous manner, but shall neuer be able to prooue their accusation: for there is no Ministrie in England ordained by the Pope or for the Pope. The Ministrie of publishing the Gospell and deliuering the Sacraments is not the deuice of man, but Christes ordinance: and therefore we receiue it not as theirs that deliuer it, neither doth their godlines or vngodlines make it better or worse vnto vs. The Ministrie was not vtterlie destroyed in the Poperie, for there remained the Sacrament of baptisme, howsoeuer the Catabaptists denie the same. How much is the Ministrie of Christ to bee acknowledged when it is onely to that end for which he ordained it, though the men that ordaine should be most vngodlie? This thing will more fullie appeare when we come to handle the agréement of the Brownists with the Donatists in that ranke Donatisme, affirming it to bee no Sacrament which is ministred by an open wicked man.

Thus much may suffice to shewe, that in denying the ministrie to bee Christs, they hold the same ground and arguments, and receiue the selfe same answere. And for their rayling termes, as generations of traitors, seducers, false Prophets, Iudasses, persecutors, and such like; I néed not mention the comparison of our men with them, seeing they doo in this, as in one of the chiefe vaines of their eloquence, apparantlie excell. Their basest disciples can crie out Antichrists, Baals Priests, false Prophets, seducers, and what not? But it will bée sayd, that in the matter of discipline the Donatists and Brownists are vnlike. I graunt the Donatists, that euer I haue read, did take no exception that way. That is not alone in question, but whether there were any fault, so that exception might be taken. And for this, men are to consider, that as corruption in doctrine and ceremonies did enter betimes into the Church, and growe a pace: so also the discipline or externall gouernment was of many neglected, abused and corrupted. Sundrie of the Pastors being proud and ambitious, the steppes were made for Antichrist to climbe vp, who challenged not onely an externall power ouer all other, but also a Lordship ouer the conscience. Thus much touching the first obiection.

The second difference obiected is, That the Donatists did condemne all Churches in the world: The Brownists condemne but the Churches of England. Indéed the Brownists doo affirme that they be farre from condemning all churches: and so here is an apparant difference, and a great, at the first sight, if men doo not narrowlie way and consider all matters. They knowe it is a great preiudice vnto them, if it bée found that they condemne all Churches: but wee may not looke vpon their words of deniall, but vpon the consequence of their matters. For he that shooteth an arrowe at one thing and together therewith striketh another, cannot bee sayd not to haue striken it because he had no such intent. So must wee consider whether the dart of condemnation which they haue shot at the Church of England, doo not together with the same runne through the sides of all Churches. I stand to proue it doth, and so that they are in this also full

Dona-

Donatists. But if they did not, yet they shall bee found thus farre in Donatisme, as to condemne some Churches of Christ. My first reason shall be from hence, that the Church of England is esteemed and reuerenced among the Churches as a sister, and communicated withall: and yet they all know what her faults be, in her assemblies, in her worship, in her ministrie and gouernment, in as much as they are open and apparant to them, euen as to our selues. Now, that they iustifie her as a true Church, we haue their own words: for the harmonie of confessions of the Churches, collected and set forth by the Churches of France and of the Lowe Countries, doth receiue and approue the confession of the Church of England, and call it one of the reformed Churches. Whereupon I argue thus: If the Church of England be Antichristian, and idolatrous, and worship the beast, bow downe vnto him and receiue his marke, because of the gouernment by Bishops: then the Churches which doo perfectlie knowe the same, and yet doo acknowledge her as a sister, and communicate with her, are partakers of her sinne, and so to be condemned with her. Therefore the Brownists condemning it, condemne those that iustifie it, knowing the estate. The Brownists condemne all those as persecutors of the iust, enemies of Christ, and of his kingdome, that shall hold them to be Heretickes and Schismatickes for condemning the Church of England and separating themselues. I argue thus: All the Churches which know the Church of England, and her forme of gouernment, and yet doo loue and reuerence her as a true Church of Christ, condemne those as hereticall Schismatickes which call it Antichristian and separate themselues from it. For how can the Churches as they doo esteeme the Church of England as a true sister, and yet not condemne the Brownists as wicked Schismatickes, which call it the Synagog of Sathan? Then let the Brownists shewe that the Churches haue reuoked this their former iudgement of the Church of England: or else let them answere whether they condemne not all those as no true Christians, which shall affirme them to

 be

be wicked Schismatickes for separating themselues from the assemblies of England: If they will deny that the churches esteeme our Churche as a sister, and therefore condemne them as ungodlie Schismatickes, the matter is so cléere that all men shal see them then to be impudent. It may be some Brownist will replie, that it cannot be extended unto all Churches a farre off which is verified in some that be nigh. Well, let us see then for the Churches a farre off. Doo not the Brownists condemne the Church of Geneua? They will say no. But I say they doo. For as I sayd before, will they not condemne all such as doo reiect them as wicked Schismatickes? This doth the Church of Geneua. Which I proue thus: In that the Church of Geneua doth approue the doctrine of those that haue béen and are her most learned and godlie Pastors: as Master Caluin, with whom the rest consent in doctrine. Now, touching the doctrine of Master Caluin published, whereby he condemneth the Brownists as Schismatickes, ye may reade it in fourth booke of his Institutions, and the first Chapter. It is too large to recite the whole, I will alleage but some parts. Looke uppon the seuenth section where he saith: that in the visible Church in earth, there are verie many hypocrites mingled; verie many that be ambicious, couetous, enuious, cursed speakers, some of more impure life, which tollerated for a time, either because they cannot in lawfull iudgemēt be conuinced, or else because that seueritie of discipline which ought to be, is not alwaies in force. In the ninth section he affirmeth, that the reason is somewhat diuers in esteeming priuate men and in esteeming the churches: for it may come to passe (as he saith) that wee ought to handle them as brethren, and accompt in stead of beléeuers, such as wee shall thinke utterlie unworthie the fellowship of the godlie, euen for the cōmon consent of the church, by which they are tollerated in the bodie of Christ. Wee doo not approue such by our voyce to be members of the Church; but we leaue unto them that place which they hold among the people of God, untill it be taken from them by lawfull iudgement. Then
be

he addeth, but wee must thinke otherwise of the multitude: which if it haue the Ministerie of the Word, and giue honour, if it haue the Administration of the Sacraments, no doubt it deserueth to bee accounted a Church: because it is certaine, those things are not without fruite: so wee both keepe for the Uniuersall Church her vnitie, which diuelish Spirites haue alwaies endeuored to cutte in sunder: neither doo wee defraude of their authoritie, the lawfull assemblies which are seuered according to the fitnes of places. In the tenth section hee vttereth that the Lord maketh so great account of the communion of his Church, that he esteemeth him as a runnagate, and forsaker of religion, whosoeuer he be that frowardlie shall separate himselfe from any Christian societie, which imbraseth but the true Ministrie of the word and Sacraments. And a little after he inferreth vpon some ground of reason, that the departure from the Church is the deniall of God and of Christ: affirming moreouer that no crime can bée deuised more horrible than with sacrilegious trecherie, to violate the mariage which the Sonne of God hath vouchsafed to contract with vs. In the twelft section hée dooth expounde what is his meaning when he requireth a pure Ministerie of the word, and pure order of administring the Sacraments, as notes infallible of the true Church. For hee saieth there may somewhat that is faltie créepe in, either in the administration of the word, or of the Sacraments, which ought not to separate vs from the Communion of that Ministrie. Because there be principles of Religion, without which we cannot be saued, and there be points in which men dissent, and the one part erreth, and yet the vnitie of faith and brotherlie loue is kept: not that we are to approue the least errour in doctrine, or the smalest corruption in the administration of the Sacraments. In the thirtéenth section he saith, that in tolerating the imperfection of life, wée ought to bée much more fauorable: for here we are vpon slipperie ground where wée may easely fall. And the euill dooth héere lie in waite, and assalt vs with speciall engines; for there haue been

been alwaies some, which being caried with a false perswasion of an absolute perfection, as if they were now become certaine ayrie spirites despised the fellowship of all men, in whome they saw any thing that is humaine or corrupt remaining. Such were of olde time the Cathari, and the Donatists which fell into the same furie: such are at this daye some of the Anabaptists which would seeme to haue profited more than others: There be other some that offend rather of an inconsiderate zeale of righteousnes than of that mad pride: for while they see the life is not answerable to the holie doctrine in bringing forth good fruite among such as haue the Gospell preached, they iudge by and by that there is no Church. Then he sheweth further that the offence is iust, and God must needs punish that there is such wounding of weake consciences: but in this they offend, as hee saieth, that they knowe not how to keepe anie measure in being offended; or omitting that clemencie which the Lord requireth, they giue themselues wholie unto immoderate seueritie. And because they think there is no Church, where there is not found puritie and integritie of life, through the hatred of wickednes they depart away from the lawfull Church, while they thinke they turne a side from the faction of the wicked. Then he proceedeth in answering their obiections, they alleage that the Church of Christ is holie; he willeth them also to understand by the parables in the Gospell, that the good and the bad are mixed together. They crie out that it is a thing intollerable that the contagious pestilence of vices doth in such violent raging sort ouerspread all, hee setteth before them the vices that were in the Churches of Corinth and Galatia. They obiect that Paul doth will we eate not with anie called a brother which is of an ungodlie life. Yea here they crie out that if it be not lawfull to eate common bread with such, how should it be lawfull to eate with them the bread of the Lord? He answereth that it is a great reproach in deede, if dogges and swine bee admitted to haue place among the children of God: yea it is also much greater, if the sacred bodie of Christ be prostituted

unto

vnto them. And where the Churches are well ordred, they doo not keepe in their bosome the notorious wicked, nor admit all without difference to that holie banquet: but the pastors are not alwaies diligent, sometime they fauour more than they ought or bee more remisse. And sometime they cannot but are letted from exercising that seueritie which they would. Now when the Church ceaseth to doo her duetie herein, it is not for euery priuate man (saith he) to separate himselfe: euery godly man is indeede to keepe himselfe from the fellowship of sinne; but it is one thing to eschewe the fellowship of sinne, and another for hatred thereof to renounce the Communion of the Church. Then hee answereth further, that Saint Paul willeth euerie one to examine himselfe when hee commeth to eate of that bread; and if it were a wicked thing to communicate with the vnworthie, Paul would certainelie haue willed vs to looke about least there should bee some in the multitude, by whose vncleannes we might be defiled. These things he hath in the fourteenth and fifteenth sections: in the sixteenth section hauing shewed that the chiefe ringleaders in such separation are led with pride, he willeth the godlie to consider that in a great multitude there are manie which are truelie, holie and innocent before the eyes of the Lord, which are hid from their sight; that of those which seeme diseased or infected, there are manie which doo not please or flatter themselues in their vices, but being eftsones awakened with an earnest feare of God labour to amend. That they must not iudge of a man for one fact: when the holiest men doo sometime fall most grieuouslie: That the Ministrie of the word, and the participation of the Sacraments, haue more force to gather a Church, than that by the fault of certaine wicked men, that whole power may vanish or come to none effect. Finallie let them consider that in esteeming a Church, the iudgement of God, is of more waight and certaintie, than the iudgement of man. In the eighteenth section, hee setteth forth how the holie Prophets of God did not separate themselues, in those horrible and lamentable desolations which they describe: when most of the people and the Priestes themselues were openlie wicked.

Thus may wee see that Master Caluine condemning the Brownists so seuerelie by the Scriptures, they must either reuoke Brownisme in this point, that the bad pollute the good, and therefore separation to be made, which he termeth sacrilegious treacherie; or else condemne him not onelie with the Church of Geneua which he taught, but also all other Churches that imbrace his writings, and acknowledge him for a noble instrument of God. Furthermore let the Brownists shew any one assemblie at this day in the World, in which there bee not open sinners admitted to the Lords table, and which sinne in great sinnes, as either in pride, selfe loue, ambition, couetousnes, idlenes, hatred, enuie, contention, backbiting, lying and in such like. They say all are polluted and fallen away from the couenant, where any that openlie sinneth is admitted to the holie Communion. How can they say then that they doo not condemne all Churches vnder heauen? Finallie when in their writings they affirme that prescript forme of prayer imposed is Idolatrie, a bondage breaking christian libertie, a thing most detestable, they doo so farre condemne all Churches, in as much as there is no one which hath not prescript forme of Prayer imposed. And the Brownist which hath published in Print, a defence of the same, alleageth the extreame curse against those that adde to Gods word Reuel.22. and saith they adde which make Lawes in the Chnrch, in matters of circumstance, or things indifferent. Which in deede all the Churches doo; and therefore hee layeth that extreame curse vpon all the reformed Churches: let no man therefore be so simple, as to imagine that the Brownists doo condemne but the English Churches, when their extreame seueritie in condemning reacheth ouer all.

Now to the third thing obiected wherein they may seeme to differ from the Donatists: namely that the Donatists did holde that the Sacraments, or the efficacie of them doth de-

pend

pend vpon the worthines of the minister: but the Brownists are not of that minde. I answere that in this great and ranck poynt of Donatisme I can find no difference at all betwéen them and the Brownists: and let the wordes and meaning of both be scanned, and it shal appeare manifestly that they hold the selfe same thing, neither more nor lesse like euen brethren.

The Brownists affirme that we haue neither worde of God nor Sacraments in our Church. But demaund of them, doth the Sacrament or the efficacie thereof depend vpon the worthines of the minister? They will aunswere, it doth not, but yet it can be no Sacrament of Christ vnles hee be a minister of Christ that doth deliuer it. If it bee saide vnto them Iudas was a most wicked man, and our Sauiour calleth him a diuell yet was he a minister of Christ for the time, and the baptisme he administred as effectual as the baptisme of any other. They will replie and say, that was so because the sinne of Iudas was secret, they were not polluted by his vncleannes, because they did not know it: But he that is an open sinner cannot be a minister of Christ; and such as receiue the Sacrament at his hand, knowing his wickednes cannot but be partakers of his sinne and polluted by the same. This wil they say is not to make either the being of a Sacrament, or the efficacie therof to depend vpon a man, but vpon Gods ordinance that he be a minster that deliuer it. I will not denie that he must be a minister that doth deliuer it: And I say withall that although the Donatists may seeme by some of their speeches to holde a further thing touching this matter, yet lay al their sayings together, and it is manifest they held, that where the sinne was secret in him that did administer, the Sacrament deliuered by him was effectuall, notwithstanding he were neuer so wicked inwardly: but if his sinne were open, he was no minister, and so no Sacrament, but the partie that communicateth with him is polluted by him.

Petilian the Donatist Bishop in the beginning of his epistle denying that they did rebaptize, but that such as were baptized in the Churches were not baptized at all, before they baptized them, for confirmation vseth this saying, *Consciētia namque dantis attenditur, quæ abluat accipientis.* For the conscience of him that giueth is attended, which may wash the conscience of him that receiueth. Further he saith, *Qui fidem a perfido sumpserit, non fidem percipit sed reatum.* He that will take faith of the faithlesse, receiueth not faith but guiltines. And rendring a reason for confirmation he saith, *Omnis enim res origine et radice consistit: & si caput non habet aliquid, nihil est.* For euery thing doth consist of an originall and roote: and if any thing haue not a head; it is nothing. Augustine answereth to these sayings of Petilian, demanding first, what if the conscience of him that giueth be secret, and perhaps vncleane, how can it wash the conscience of him that receiueth? For if the Donatist shall say it apperteineth not to the receiuer, whatsoeuer euill lie hid in the conscience of the giuer, that ignorance perhaps shal be of this force, that vnwittinglie he cannot bee defiled by the conscience of him that baptizeth him: let it suffice therefore that the defiled conscience of an other while it is not knowne doth not pollute, yet will they say it shall also wash? From whence is he washed then that receiueth baptisme of one that hath a polluted conscience, and he doth not knowe so much? Séeing he saith, he that will take faith of him that is faithles, doth not receiue faith, but guiltines. Behold a faithles man doth stand to baptize, but he that is to be baptized doth not knowe his vnfaithfulnes, what doest thou thinke he shall receiue, faith or guiltines? If the Donatist say, he receiueth faith, then he inferreth, that it is graunted it may come to passe, that a man may receiue faith and not guiltines from an vnfaithful man, and so the former saying is false. But if the Donatist should answere, he receiueth guiltines: then he saith the Donatists should baptize those againe which were baptized among themselues by wicked men, whose wickednesse was secrete at such time as they did baptize, but afterward they were bewraied, conuict, and condemned. I say then it is manifest by the

the practise of the Donatists, in not baptizing againe any of those which had been among them baptized by their owne Ministers whom they esteemed godlie, but afterward were disclosed to be ranke hypocrites, and so they condemned and cast them forth, that their iudgement was, that he was a Minister of Christ, though a reprobate touching his owne person, and the Sacrament deliuered by him a true Sacrament, so long as his wickednes lay hid from the knowledge of men: howsoeuer the reasons of Petilian which he vttered in the rash heate of his furie, may seeme to stretch further. And where as Augustine answering to ẏ rest of the words saith: *Quapropter siue à fideli, siue à perfido dispensatore Sacramentum baptismi quisque percipiat, spes ei omnis in Christo sit, ne sit maledictus qui spem suam ponit in homine. Alioquin si talis quisq; in gratia spirituali renascitur, qualis est ille à quo baptizatur, & cum manifestus est qui baptizat homo bonus, ipse dat fidem, ipse origo & radix, capútq; nascentis est: cùm autem latet perfidus baptizator, tunc quisque à Christo percipit fidem, tunc à Christo ducit originem, tunc in Christo radicatur, tunc Christo capite gloriatur: laborandum est omnibus qui baptizantur vt baptizatores perfidos habeant, & ignorent eos.* That is to say: Wherefore whosoeuer receiueth the Sacrament of baptisme, whether it bee of a faithfull, or whether it be of an vnfaithfull dispensor, let all his hope be in Christ, least he be accursed as one that putteth his trust in man. Otherwise if euerie one that is borne in spirituall grace be such an one, as he is by whom he is baptized: and when he that baptizeth is manifest a good man, he giueth faith, he is the originall, the roote and the head of him that is newe borne: but when he that baptizeth is vnfaithfull being not knowne so to be, then euerie one receiueth faith of Christ, taketh originall from Christ, is rooted in Christ and glorieth in Christ his head: then all men are to endeuour which are baptized, that they may haue vnfaithfull baptizers, so they knowe them not to be such. His reason is, that when the man that baptizeth is secretlie wicked, it is most absurd to say his conscience baptizeth, or that he is the roote or head of him that is regenerate, and therefore the Donatists confessing such to bee truelie baptized, he saith it must néeds then be Christ that doth baptize. And thereupon inferreth, that this absurditie must needes followe, which is most foolish to beléeue, that it is better to be baptized of a secret wicked man, than of the best manifest godlie man, because Christ is incomparablie better than the best men. Wherefore he wisheth them to confesse whether the Minister be good or bad, it is Christ alone that doth baptize, that giueth faith, that is the roote and the head. It will now be said, that by this it appeareth the Donatists did ascribe all to the man, if he were godlie. Let vs see therefore what they answere. Cresconius taking vpon him to defend the saying of Petilian, in this that the conscience of the giuer doth wash the conscience of the receiuer: and Augustine demaunded, what if the giuer be of a defiled conscience, and secret? Cresconius answereth: *Conscientia dantis attenditur, non secundum eius synceritatem, quae in illa videri non potest, sed secundum famam quae de illa seu vera, seu falsa est: quia videlicet eius est hominis, qui & si sceleratus occultus sit, sufficit accipienti, quod bonae sit existimationis nondum cognitus, nondum iudicatus, nondum ab ecclesia separatus.* That is, The conscience of the giuer is attended, not according to the synceritie thereof, which in it cannot be seene, but according to the fame which is of it whether true or false: that is to say, because it is of that mã, who though he be secretlie wicked, it is sufficient for the receiuer, that he is of good estimatio, not yet knowne, not yet iudged, not yet separate from the Church. Booke. 2. Chapt. 17. This blind shift had Cresconius alleaged to auoide those former absurdities, and fell into as great that false fame doth baptize. By which it appeareth that the whole matter of the Donatists opinion rested in this, that an open wicked man onely did not, or could not baptize. Cresconius calleth vpon Augustine thus: *Responde quomodo baptizent quos damnauit ecclesia?* Answere how they can baptize whom the Church hath condemned? Augustine doth answere: *Sic eos baptizare, quomodo bapti-*

zant quos damnauit Deus, antequam de illis quicquam iudicaret ecclesia. That they baptize as those doo whom GOD hath cōdemned, before the Church hath iudged any thing of them. And seeing the secrete wicked man is condemned alreadie by Christ, and the Church is subiect to Christ: hée inferreth, *Non igitur debet ecclesia se Christo praeponere, vt putet baptizare posse ab illo iudicatos, à se autem iudicatos baptizare non posse, cum ille semper veraciter iudicet, ecclesiastici autem Iudices sicut homines plerunque falluntur.* Therefore the Church ought not to preferre her selfe before Christ, as to thinke that such as are condemned by him can baptize, but such as are condemned by her cannot baptize, when he alwaies iudgeth truely, where the ecclesiasticall Iudges as men are oftentimes deceiued. Hereupon hee concludeth, *Baptizant ergo quantum attinet ad visibile ministerium, & boni, & mali, inuisibiliter autem per eos baptizat, cuius est & visibile baptisma, & inuisibilis gratia. Tingere ergo possunt & boni & mali, abluere autem conscientiam non nisi ille, qui semper est bonus.* Therefore both the good and the bad do baptize in as much as appertaineth to the visible ministrie, but inuisiblie by them doth hee baptize whose is both the visible baptisme, and also the inuisible grace. Both the good then and the bad may dippe them in the water, but to wash the cōscience, there can none but he which is alwaies good. Booke. 2. Chapt. 21. Cresconius procéedeth, demaunding what can be vttered more wicked than this, *Vt purificet aliū maculosus, abluat sordidus, emundet immundus, det infidelis fidem, criminosus faciat innocentem.* That he which is spotted should purifie another, he that is foule should wash, he that is vncleane should clense, that an Infidell should giue faith, that he which is criminous should make another innocent? Booke. 3. Chapt. 5. Augustine answereth: *Nec maculosus, nec sordidus, nec immundus, nec infidelis, nec criminosus est Christus, qui dilexit ecclesiam & seipsum tradidit pro ea, mundans eam lauacro aquae in verbo, faciens nos certos de bonis suis, ne malis viciaremur alienis.* Christ is not spotted, nor foule, nor vncleane, nor an infidell, nor criminous

which

which hath loued his Church and giuen himselfe for it cleansing it by the lauer of water through the word, making vs sure of his good things, that wee cannot be defiled with the euill of other men.

But now to come to a more cleere opening of this matter, whereas Petilian had saide that euerie thing consisteth of an originall and roote, and if any thing haue not an head it is nothing: and the answere was made, that Christ is the originall, the roote and the head of him that is baptized: and that he is accursed which putteth his trust in man. Cresconius doth replie, as Augustine reporteth his words, *Hoc & nos suademus & volumus, vt semper Christus det fidem, Christus sit origo Christiani, in Christo radicem Christianus infigat, Christus Christiani sit caput. Non quærimus hominem in quo spem constituat accepturus, sed quærimus per quem hoc melius fiat? Et quia sine ministro nec vos dicitis hominem posse baptizari, quærimus vtrúmne melius iniustus sit minister, an iustus?* This also (saieth the Donatists) we will and perswade, that Christ alwaies giueth faith, Christ is the originall of a Christian, in Christ the Christian must fixe his roote, that Christ is the head of the Christian, wee seeke not a man in whome he that is to be baptized may set his hope, but we seeke by whome this may better be done. And because you also say a man cannot be baptized without a minister, we demaund whether is the better, that the minister be vniust, or that he be iust. Booke 3. chapt. 6, 7, and 8. Augustine replieth. *Vbi respondeo, ad hoc esse melius, vt sit iustus minister, quod infirmitas hominis, cui sine exemplo laboriosum est & difficile quod imperat Deus, imitatione boni ministri ad vitam bonam facilius erigatur. Vnde dicit Apostolus Paulus, imitatores mei estote, sicut & ego Christi. ad hominem vero baptizandum, & sanctificandum, si tantò est melius quod accipitur, quantò est melior per quem traditur: tanta est in accipientibus baptismorum varietas, quanta in ministris diuersitas meritorum. Si enim, quod sine controuersia creditur, melior erat Paulus quam Apollo, meliorem baptismum profectò dedit, secundùm istam vestram vanam*

peruer-

peruersamque sententiam. Et si meliorem baptismum dedit, profecto eis quos a se non baptizatos gratulatur inuidit. Porro si inter bonos ministros, cum sit alius alio melior, non est melior baptismus qui per meliorem datur, nullo modo est malus qui etiam per malum datur, quando idem baptismus datur, & ideo per ministros dispares, Dei munus aequale est, quia non illorum, sed eius est. Where I answere (saith Augustine) That in this respect it is better, that the minister be godly, because the infirmitie of man, to whome without an example it is laboursome and difficult to doo that which God commaundeth, may more easilie by the imitation of a good minister be raised vp and supported vnto good life. Whereupon the Apostle Paul saieth, *Be yee followers of me, as I am of Christ*. But for the Baptizing, and sanctifying a man, If it be so much better which is receiued, as he is better, by whome it is deliuered: then there is as great varietie of Baptismes in the receiuers, as there is diuersitie of worthines in the ministers. For if Paul were better than Apollo, which is beleeued without controuersie, then hee vereli, according to that your vaine and peruerse sentence, gaue a better baptisme. And if he deliuered a better baptisme, doubtles he enuied those for whome hee is glad that they were not baptized by him. Moreouer if it be so, that among the good Ministers, when one is better than another, the baptisme is not better which is deliuered by the better, it is by no meane euill when it is giuen by a naughtie man, seeing the same baptisme is deliuered. And therefore by vnequall Ministers, the gift of God is equall, because it is his, and not theirs. Thus farre Augustine. It is apparant enough by that which I haue alreadie cited, what the Donatists meant in denying it to bee Baptisme which was administred by an open wicked man: and requiring for the trueth and efficacie of Baptisme, that it should be administred by a godlie man, or at the least by a man godlie in shew: but yet I will adde somewhat more. Petilian replying vpon Augustine with great railing, saide also that those absurdities which he gathered were his own. booke 3. chap. 45. And

45. And whereas Augustine had demaunded, what if the conscience of him that deliuereth be vncleane & secret, what doth wash (if anie thing be to be that way regarded in mā)? he answereth it is as to say, *Quid si nunc cœlum ruat?* What if the skie shuld now fal? Moreouer he saith that two words of his were omitted by Augustine, in his two sayings: the one is, the conscience of him that giueth, where he saieth his words were *sanctè dantis*, of him that giueth holilie: The other, he that will take faith of an vnfaithfull man, hee receiueth not faith but guiltines: where hee saith this word *sciens*, was omitted: which is knowing. So that howsoeuer Petilian séemed in his heate to vtter otherwise, hee will haue this to be his meaning, that hee which receiueth Baptisme of a Minister whome he knoweth to be a wicked man, because his sinnes are open, he receiueth not Baptisme, but pollution and guiltines, by Communicating with him. booke 3. Chapter 31. Againe, where Petilian and the rest affirmed, that hee which is Baptized of one that is dead, his washing doth not profit him, hee meaneth by one that is dead, not the secret wicked, nor yet the open sinner, vntill the Church haue condemned him Booke 1. Chap. 10. Parmenian that Donatist Bishop, to proue that it was no Baptisme which was ministred by an open wicked man, alleageth that the wicked which sacrificeth a shéepe, is as hee that cutteth off the head of a dog; and the sacrifice of the wicked is an abomination to the Lord. Esay. 66. And that the man which had any blemish, or spot in him should not come to offer as a Priest to the Lord Leuit. 21. And that God heareth not sinners. Iohn. 9. As Augustine reporteth against Parmenian Booke 2. Chapt. 6, 7, 8. Where Augustine answereth, *Vnicuique retribuit Deus secundùm cor suum. Nam si primis temporibus non obfuerunt mali sacerdotes, vel collegis bonis, sicut fuit Zacharias: vel popularibus, sicut fuit Nathaniel in quo dolus non erat, quantò magis nihil obest in Christiana vnitate Episcopus malus, vel coepiscopis vel laicis bonis, cùm iam ille sacerdos in æternum secundùm ordinem Melchisedech & pontifex noster sedens ad dextram patris, interpel-*

interpellat pro nobis,&c. God rendreth vnto euerie one according to his heart. For if in the first times, the naughtie Priests did not hurt either their fellowes which were good, such as was Zacharie: or anie of the people, such as was Nathaniel, in whom was no guile. How much more doth an euill Bishop in the Christian vnitie, nothing hurt, either his fellowe Bishops being good, or anie of the laietie? when now that Priest for euer after the order of Melchisedech, euen our high Priest, sitting at the right hand of the Father, maketh intercession for vs, &c. *Dicant ergo mihi, cui sancto secundùm salutem spiritualem obfuerit vel in sacerdotibus, vel inter populum constituto, malus aut maculatus sacerdos?* Let them shew vnto me therefore which holie one either of the Priests or among the people, an euill and spotted Priest did hurt touching spirituall saluation. Where was Moses and Aaron, there were the wicked murmurers: where was Caiphas and other such like, there were Zacharie, Symeon and other godlie ones: where Saul was, there was Dauid; where Esay, Ieremie, Ezechiel, and Daniel were, there were the wicked Priests, and naughtie people. *Sed sarcinam suam vnusquisque portabat.* But euerie one did beare his owne burthen. And hauing shewed that the words of Balaam a wicked man were heard of God for the people, he addeth, *Vnde non mirum est, verba bona quæ pro populo dicũtur in precibus, etiam si a malis dicantur episcopis, exaudiri tamen, non pro peruersitate præpositorum, sed pro deuotione populorum.* From whence it is no meruaile, that good words which are vttered in prayer for the people are heard, though they bee vttered by naughtie Bishops, not for the peruersenes of the guides, but for the deuotion of the people. No man can take any thing vnles it be giuen him from aboue; Petilian saith thereupon: *Doce igitur traditor simulandi mysteria quando acceperis potestatem,* Shew therefore thou Traitor, when thou diddest receiue the power of counterfaiting the mysteries. Booke 2. Chapter. 31. Hee termeth it a counterfaiting, or faining of the sacraments when they bee ministred by one that is openlie wicked, because he holdeth, that God neuer authorised any such to deliuer them. And what is the whole pith of Brownists touching this poynt, when they crie out that wee haue no word of God, nor Sacraments, but euen the verie same that the Donatists held, namelie that if he be openlie wicked, because God commaundeth there should be no such in the Ministerie, he hath no authoritie to Baptize, and so it is no Sacrament which is deliuered by them: The Brownists affirme that the efficacie is of God, the faith is of God, the grace is of God alone, but God bestoweth these by such onelie as be his true Ministers, and those are none that be openlie wicked. The Donatists did affirme nothing but the verie same: For Augustine thus rehearseth the words of Cresconius, *Ideo magis te dicis iustum & fidelem, per quem hoc sacramentum celebretur inquirere, quia spem & fiduciam Dei non hominis habes: Dei esse autem fidem atque iustitiam, quam semper in ministris eius attendis.* Thou saiest that because thy hope and confidence is in God and not in man, thou dost so much the rather seeke for one that is iust and faithfull by whome this Sacrament may be celebrated: and that the faith and righteousnes is of God, which thou doost attend in his Ministers. Booke 3. Chap. 9. I hold him therefore a verie sharpe discerner, which waying throughlie all the sayings of the Donatists, shall be able in this poynt of hanging the being and efficacie of the Sacraments, vpon the worthines of the Ministers, to shew anie small difference betweene the Brownists and them. Yea but herein they may seeme to differ verie much, that the Donatists did rebaptize, but the Brownists doo not. In deed herein I confesse they differ, but yet so that in this difference the Brownists are the grosser, if we may reason from that which they holde: for if this were true, which the Brownists affirme most stiffelie to bee true, as the Donatists did before them, that where an open wicked man dooth administer the Sacraments they be no Sacraments at all. And if this also were as true, which they both haue taken vpon them to iustifie, the Donatists of olde saying, they had no true Sacraments

in

in the Churches, and the Brownists that we haue none now: It must needes be graunted that the Donatists did the better of both, in baptising those which were not before baptized: for he that is not baptized ought to be baptized. And as no vncircumcised might eate of the Passeouer, but was to be cut off from the people of GOD: so no vnbaptized is to eate at the table of the Lord. How grosse are the Brownists which take it as a thing vndoubted that we haue no Sacraments, and must needes thereupon be assured that they themselues were neuer baptized, and so can be but as an heape of vncircumcised, and yet seeke not to haue the Sacrament? I would haue them answer this question, whether a man that knoweth he was neuer baptized, can be saued, if he seeke not to bee baptized, when hee may come by it? Let no man imagine that I speake this as though the Brownists should doo well in rebaptizing, for their former ground is false, wicked and hereticall, when they say it is no Sacrament that hath been administred by open offenders: and that we haue no Sacraments. But if that were true which they hold, they should doo much better, I will not say to rebaptize, but to baptize such as were not before baptized.

Now, where it is generallie obiected, that the Donatists perhaps held diuers things which the Brownists doo not. I answere, that the Donatists indeede held somewhat which the Brownists doo not, and the Brownists hold something which they did not. For some of the Donatists did cast themselues downe from high places, and into the fire, accounting them holie Martyres that so died, and others defended their doing. For thus saith Gaudentius a Donatist Bishop in his Epistle, *An ista persecutio est, quæ tot millia innocentum martyrum arctauit ad mortem? Christiani enim secundum euangelium spiritu prompti, sed carne infirmi à sacrilega contaminatione caminorum reperto compendio suas animas rapuerunt, imitati presbyteri Razia in Machabæorum libris exemplum, nec frustra timentes: quisquis enim eorum manus inciderit, non euasit: sed quantum velint faciant, quod certum est, dei esse non poßunt qui faciunt contra Deum.* Whether is that

 a per-a persecution (saith he) which hath pent vp in a straight so many thousands of innocent martyres euen vnto death? For Christians according to the Gospell, being readie in spirit, but weake in the flesh, finding out a compendious way of their chimneyes, haue deliuered their soules from the sacrilegious pollution, imitating the example of olde Razia in the bookes of the Machabees, not fearing without cause: for whosoeuer falleth into their hands, doth not escape: but let them doo as much as they will, that which is certaine, they cannot be of God, which doo against God. booke 2. against Gaudent. Chapt. 20. Augustine sheweth, that Gaudentius meaning was not that they burnt themselues in their chimneys for feare of persecution vnto death, for the ciuill Magistrate did not so persecute them, hauing made a lawe against them for banishment, but not for death: as Augustine sheweth booke 2. against Gaudentius chap. 11. *Mitiora in vos constituit Imperator propter mansuetudinem Christianam: exilium vobis voluit inferre, non mortem.* The Emperour hath decreed more gentle thinges against yee through Christian mildnes: he would lay banishment vppon ye and not death. But his meaning is that such as fell into their hands were drawne to ioyne with them in worship, which he calleth the sacriligious defilement. And therfore doth abuse that place of the Gospell, to colour such horrible murthering of themselues, the spirit is readie but the flesh is weake: for fearing least through weakenes they should yeeld to ioyne with the Churches, they rather chose to kill themselues. This the Brownists doo not: but they condemne read prayer, or praying after any prescript forme of words which the Donatists did not, as may bee gathered by these words of Petilian: *Si precem domino facitis, aut funditis orationem, nihil vobis penitus prodest. Vestras enim debiles preces cruenta vestra conscientia vacuat, quia dominus deus puram magis conscientiam quam preces exaudit, domino Christo dicente, non omnis qui dicit mihi domine, domine, intrabit in regnum cœlorum, sed is qui facit voluntatem patris mei qui est in cœlis. Voluntas dei vtique bona est, nam ideo in sacra oratione*

tione sic petimus, fiat voluntas tua sicut in cœlo, & in terra. If ye make prayer to the Lord (saith the Donatist) or powre foorth supplication, it doth profite ye nothing at al, for your bloudie conscience doth make your weake prayers of none effect, because the Lord God doth rather heare a pure conscience than prayers, the Lord Iesus saying, *that not euerie one that saith vnto me Lord Lord shall enter into the kingdom of heauen, but he that doth the will of my father which is in heauen.* The will of God is good, for therefore in the holie prayer we pray thus, *thy will be done in earth as it is in heauen.* Thus we see that the Donatist denying that any praied but they, sheweth withall that praying they vsed the Lords prayer.

But what doo I stand to seeke differences betwéen them, which can hardlie be found: whereas indeede whole bookes doo set foorth at large their agreement. I will therefore proceede further to declare in particulars touching the power of Christian Princes, in reforming the Church, in establishing religion, and in punishing heretickes, schismatickes, and disturbers, and in compelling their subiects to the obedience of the trueth, or to imbrace the true worship, how iniuriouslie Browne hath dealt in his booke, and the Brownists that haue written since, I haue layd open in my former booke, let their sayings be throughlie perused, and now shall ye seee a little whether they be not the verie naturall children of the Donatists in this poynt also. Thus writeth Gaudentius a Donatist Bishop: *Per opificem rerum omnium dominum Christum omnipotens deus frabricatum hominem vt deo similem, libero dimisit arbitrio. Scriptum est enim, fecit deus hominem & dimisit eum in manu arbitrij sui. Quid mihi nunc humano imperio eripitur quod largitus est deus? Aduerte vir summe quanta in deum sacrilegia perpetrentur, vt quod ille tribuit auferat humana præsumptio, & pro deo se inaniter iactet magna iniuria dei, si ab hominibus defendatur. Quid de deo æstimat qui eum violentia vult defendere, nisi quia non valet suas ipse iniurias vindicare?* God almightie (saith this Donatist) by the maker of all thinges the Lord Christ, left man to his owne

free

free will being created as in the likenes of GOD. For it is written, God made man and left him in the power of his owne will. Why should that bee plucked from me by humane authoritie, which GOD hath bestowed vpon me? Marke most worthie man, how great sacrileges are committed against God, that humane presumption should take that away which he hath giuen, and vainly boast it selfe for God with great iniurie to God, if he must be defended by men. What doth he esteeme of God, which will defend him with violence, but that he is not able to reuenge the iniuries done vnto him? In what sense this Donatist spake thus, may best appeare by the answere of Augustine. *Secundum illas vestras fallacissimas vanissimásq; rationes, habenis laxatis atq; dimissis, humanæ licentiæ impunita peccata omnia relinquentur nullis oppositis repagulis legum, nocendi audacia, & lasciuiendi libido bacchetur, non rex suum regnum, non dux militem, non prouincialem iudex, non dominus seruum, nec pater filium à libertate & suauitate peccandi minis vllis pœnisue compescat. Auferte quod sana doctrina pro sanitate orbis terrarum sapienter per Apostolorum dicit, & vt confirmetis in arbitrio tanto peiore quanto liberiore filios perditionis, delete quod ait vas electionis, omnis anima potestatibus sublimioribus, subdita sit: non est enim potestas nisi à deo. Quæ autem à deo sunt, ordinata sunt. Quapropter qui resistit potestati, dei ordinationi resistit. Qui autem resistunt, ipsi sibi iudicium acquirunt. Principes enim non sunt timori boni operis, sed mali. Vis autem non timere potestatem? Fac bonum, & habebis laudẽ ex illa. Dei enim minister est, vindex in iram ei qui male agit. Delete ista si potestis, aut ista, sicut facitis, si non potestis delere, cõtemnite. Habete de his omnibus pessimum arbitriũ, ne perdatis liberũ arbitriũ, aut certe quia sicut homines hominibus erubescitis, clamate si audetis, puniãtur homicidia, puniantur adulteria, puniantur cætera quãtalibet sceleris, siue libidinis facinora seu flagitia sola sacrilegia volumus à regnantiũ legibus impunita. An verò aliud dicitis, cũ dicitis, magna dei iniuria si ab hominibus defendatur. Quid de deo æstimat qui eũ violẽtia vult defendere, nisi quia nõ valet suas ipse iniurias vindicare?*

Hæc

Hac dicentes, quid aliud dicitis, nisi nulla hominis potestas cõtradicat atque obstrepat nostro libero arbitrio, quando iniuriam facimus deo. **That is,** According to these your most deceiuable & most vaine reasons, the raines being let loose to humane licentiousnes, all sinnes shall be let goe vnpunished, no barres of lawes opposed, the boldnes to hurt, and lust of rioting shall rage euery where, the King shall not with any threatnings or penalties restraine his kingdome, nor the Captaine the souldier, nor the Iudge any of his circuit, nor the master his seruant, nor the father his sonne from the libertie and sweetnes of sinning. Take away that which sound doctrine, for the health of the world saith wiselie by the Apostle, and that ye may confirme the children of perdition in a will, by how much the more free, by so much the worse, blot out that which the elect vessell saith; *Let euerie soule be subiect to the higher powers: for there is no power but of God. The powers that bee are ordained of God. Wherefore he that resisteth the power, resisteth the ordinance of God: and they that resist shall receiue to themselues damnation. For Princes are not a terrour for well dooing but for euill. Wilt thou not feare the power? Doo well and thou shalt haue praise of it: for he is the minister of God for wrath to take vengeance vpon the euill doer.* Blot out these things if ye can, or else as ye doo, despise these thinges, because ye cannot blot them out. Haue a will concerning al these things most euill, that ye may not lose your free will. Or verely, because as men ye are ashamed before men, crie out if ye dare, let murtherers be punished, let adulteries bee punished, let other whatsoeuer enormities & hainous deeds of wickednes & lust be punished, wee will that only sacrilegies go vnpunished by the lawes of princes. Do ye say any other thing, when ye say, it is great iniurie to God, that he should be defended by men? What doth he esteeme of God which will defend him with violence, but that he is not able to reuẽge the iniuries done to him? saying these things, what other thing say yee, but that no power of man must gainsay or mutter against our free will when we doo iniurie to God?

Thus farre Augustine: But let us see further what Gaudentius saith, *Sed bellifera pacis cruentaque vnitatis se incolas iactant, audiant Dominum dicentem, pacem meam do vobis, pacem relinquo vobis: non sicut seculum dat, ego do vobis. Seculi enim pax inter animos gentium dissidentes armis & belli exitu fœderatur: domini Christi pax, salubri lenitate tranquilla, volentes inuitat non cogit inuitos.* But they boast themselues (saieth the Donatist) as inhabitants of warring peace, and bloudie vnitie. Let them heare the Lord, saying, *My peace I giue vnto yee, my peace I leaue vnto ye: not as the world giueth, doo I giue.* For the peace of the world, when the minds of the Nations are at discord, is couenanted or established with armour and euent of warre: The peace of the Lord Christ being calme with healthfull lenitie inuiteth the willing, compelleth not the vnwilling. This Donatist addeth, *Ad docendum populum Israel omnipotens Deus prophetis præconium dedit, non regibus imperauit. Saluator animarum Dominus Christus, ad insinuandam fidem, piscatores, non milites misit.* To teach the people of Israel almightie God gaue prophets to preach, he inioyned not Kings. The sauiour of Soules the Lord Christ, to insinuate faith sent fishers and not Souldiers. Booke 2. against Gaudentius chapt. 11. 16. 26.

Let us see also what Petillian that other Donatist Bishop saith, booke 2. against him Chapter 78. *Charitas non persequitur non aduersus cæteras animas Imperatores inflammat.* Charity doth not persecute it doth not inflame or kindle the wrath of rulers against others. This was the out-crie of the Donatists against the godly teachers of the churches when the Emperours made any lawes to driue them from their madnes, that they had inflamed the rulers to persecute them. *Iesus Christus ita fidem venerat facere, non vt cogeret homines, sed potius inuitaret.* Iesus Christ came so to worke faith, not that hee might compell men, but rather inuite them. *Quodsi cogi per legem aliquem vel ad bona licuisset, vosipsi miseri a nobis ad fidem purissimam cogi debuistis. Sed absit, absit a nostra conscientia, vt ad nostram fidem aliquem*

com-

compellamus. If it were lawfull (saith this Donatist) that anie should by the Lawe be compelled, yea euen vnto good things, you wretches ought to bee compelled by vs, to the most pure faith: but farre be it, farre be it, from our conscience, that we should compell anie vnto our faith. chapt. 83. *Quid vobis est cum regibus seculi quos nunquam Christianitas nisi inuidos sensit?* What haue you to doo with the Kings of the Worlde which the Christianitie hath neuer felt but enuious against it? Chapter. 92. Compare now the doctrine of our Brownists and their sayings with these former of the Donatists, and see if there bee anie difference? They say Princes are not to make Lawes for Church matters, Princes are not to reforme the Church by their authoritie: Princes are not to compell their subiects to the true worship of God by penalties: If Princes pleasures are to be attended, where is the persecution wee speake of? None of the godlie Kings of Iudea durst compell anie to the couenant. The people of Christs Kingdome are *spontanei*, such as come of their owne free accord, &c. It were too long and tedious, to set foorth all the outcries of the Donatists, their glorying in suffering persecutions for the trueth, their accusations against the pastors of Christs Churche and the Princes while they sought to restraine their furie, the one by Gods word, the other by lawes; that they persecuted, and therefore could not be the true Church which as they say is persecuted, but neuer persecuteth: reade the epistle of Parmenian, of Petilian, and of Cresconius. The Brownists are not behinde them an inch in this matter, but crie out as fast of Antichristian persecutors, boasting of their patience and sufferings, calling themselues the persecuted remnant, the poore afflicted, &c. Aug. answereth those Donatists at large, I will recite but a litle. *Cum phreneticus medicum vexet, & medicus phreneticum liget, aut ambo inuicem persequuntur, aut si persecutio quæ malo fit, non est, non vtiq; persequitur medicus phreneticum, sed phreneticus medicum.* When the man that is in phrensie dooth vex the phisitian, and the phisitian dooth binde him that is in phrensie, ei-

ther

ther both doo persecute each other, or else if that bee not a persecution which is done to the euill, then verelie the phisitian dooth not persecute the phrantick or mad man, but the phrantick or mad man dooth persecute the phisitian. Against Cresconius Booke 4. Chapter. 51. his application is that the penall Lawes of the Princes were as the bands of the Phisitian to binde the Phrensie and furious outrage of the Donatists. And whereas they boasted of patience, and woulde compell none. He answereth, that because they bee not able to resist so manie nations which were Catholike, they gloried of patience, that they compelled none to their part. Hee then addeth, *Isto modo & miluus cum pullos rapere territus non potuerit, columbum se nominet.* After the same sort the Puttocke when he is fraid and can not snatch away the chickens, may name himselfe a Doue. For he doth demaund of them what they haue not done which they were able? When Iulian the Apostata being Emperour, & enuying the peace of Christ, shewed them fauour, and graunted to them Churches, what slaughters they committed? Likewise he sheweth in many places what reuell their circumcellions made, which in companies walking with clubbes and staues did spoile, and beate such as light into their handes, vsing moreouer a sauage crueltie in putting vineger and lime into mens eies when they had beaten them. And verely what is it which men of exceeding intemperate heate will not doe, if it bee once in their power against such as they shall iudge to bee but as vile Idolaters and persecutors of Christes truth.

The impatient heate of most Brownistes is not vnknowe, but when the Kites for feare can not snatch vp the Chickens, must professe the mekenes of Doues; as to say we are Christes poore afflicted seruants, we be meeke and patient, we beare the crosse. Where it is taught that priuate men are authorised to deale, and furie aboundeth, which things are among the Brownistes: who is able to expresse the tragedies that would ensue, if power were not wanting in them: the Princes may not stoppe their course, and who shall then resist?

resist: The Donatists abusing the scriptures in their plentifull allegations, and finding that their grosenesse was detected much by the skill of artes, found fault that any thing should be scanned by the rules of Logike. The Brownistes are euen with them, if not beyond. In his first booke against Cresconius Chap. 14: Augustine reporteth the wordes of that Donatist thus: *Vestros Episcopos laudas quod nobiscum velut dialecticis nolint habere sermonem*. Thou doest commend your Bishoppes, that they refuse to haue speech or conference with vs as being Logicians. He answereth at large in shewing what Logicke is, and the worthie and necessarie vse thereof in discussing matters of religion. Browne in the preface of his booke which (hee saith) sheweth the life and manners of Christians, calleth them sophisticall diuines which deale by the rules of Logicke. The Brownistes with whome I deale, charge the students of the Uniuersities, as trained vp in vaine and curious Artes. And what other cause shall euer be shewed of so barbarous an errour, but that they would not haue their matters tried by the rules which make manifest which is truth, and which is falsehoode. Thus haue I briefely laide open that the whole Donatisme is maintained by the Brownistes, and therefore I haue rightly termed them the Donatistes of England.

An answere to Master Greene-wood, touching read prayer.

Master Greenewood in the preface of his booke, dooth shew, that the reasons spread abroade in writing against read praier were his, which I did not knowe before now, and therefore hee taketh upon him the defence of them. He would seeme to haue found out such a deapth of spirituall wisdome touching the holie exercise of prayer, and so reprooueth the grosenes of this age, that wee must esteeme him for the aboundance of spirit, as an other Montanus. For whereas hee seemeth to charge this age onelie as grosse in this poynt, in verie deede he accuseth all ages, all Churches, and all the learned teachers that haue beene since the Apostles; so that in the gifts of the spirite he excelleth all. Hee saieth hee could yet neuer see it set downe, which is the true praier that onelie pleaseth God. It is a strange thing hee hath neuer heard, that whosoeuer asketh in faith, whether it be with prescript forme, or otherwise it is the onelie true praier that pleaseth God. Hee saieth I haue flien upon him with bitternesse of spirite and carnall wisdome, loding him and the faithfull with opprobrious titles. It is to no purpose that I should answer againe with words, but when men shall once see throughlie into the fowlnes and dangers of Brownisme, and what filthie geare they spread abroade, they will thinke it requisite and necessarie to call a spade, a spade: Donatisme must

must bee called Donatisme, schisme must bee called schisme, and heresies and fantasies must haue their due titles. And now touching the defence he maketh, it is nothing but certaine ragges which he peeceth together to couer his nakednes, which also must be plucked from him. It seemeth he doth trust to the ignorance, or rashnes of some, which either cannot, or will not examine things aright.

God is a spirit, & to be worshipped in spirit. I did & do confesse, y^t this scripture doth cut downe all carnall worship, as disagreeing from the nature of God: & therefore may most fitlie be alleaged against such as shall maintaine that the verie bodilie action in reading is the worship of God. But it is friuolous to applie it against praying after a prescript forme: seeing a man may vpon a booke pray reading or after a prescript forme with sighes and groanes which proceed of faith. Master Greenewood termeth this a bodilie distinction. Doubtles if it be a bodilie distinction to affirme that the verie bodilie action of reading a prayer is not the worship of God (which we maintaine against the Papists in their lippe labour) I knowe not what Master Greenwood will allowe to bee spirituall. What manner of spirit is his? But now that he will put away all my distinctions by his affirming still (for those bee his wordes) and what? Euen the whole matter in question betweene vs: who cannot see what a valiant champion he is, for how falselie he saith he hath prooued, shall appeare? Then hauing stoutlie affirmed that which is in question, he saith, and yet say you to applie this scripture thus against read prayer is friuolous. How commeth in this word (yet)? Doth it follow that I do not well in saying so, notwithstanding you affirme the contrarie: but you haue a reason of great force, which is in these words, I appeale to all mens consciences for the waight thereof. Shall the consciences of all men bee made iudge whether that scripture bee rightlie applied? Nay, I appeale from the consciences of the Brownists. Now in the next words where I affirmed that a man may pray by the Spirite of GOD, with sighes and groanes vpon a booke, or when

he

he prayeth after a prescript forme, and therefore the application of that scripture is friuolous, his shiftes are as slender.
For touching this clause, that I say, (or after a prescript
forme) he saith, I goe about to alter the question at the first
steppe. For as much as all our prayers ought to be vttered
after a prescript forme, euen that perfect rule and forme our
Sauiour gaue to his disciples and all posterities. A great
peece of work. By vttering after a prescript forme, I meane
when a man hath learned a prayer eyther of the scripture,
or framed from thence, and can vtter it without the booke,
as it is written.

And whereas it can not be denied, but that many do pray
feruentlie with sighes and grones and teares, which reade
the prayer vpon the booke, or haue it as we vse to say, by
hart: He answereth that I begge the question. If a man
do proue the cause by the effects, which I doe heere, it is
no begging of the question, but a firme proofe. Where any
thing is burnt, there hath beene fire. Where there be sighes
and grones in prayer with inward comfort, there is faith,
there is Gods spirit, but these are in some that reade their
prayers vpon the booke, or vse prescript forme.

Maister Greenewood thinketh he hath disputed subtil-
lie, and couered himselfe, when he can say, ye alter the question, ye begge the question, ye assume the question.
Nowe touching the defence of his reasons he brought. If
those sighes and grones (saith he) were of faith, that
would minister matter of prayer without a booke.
This reason (as I sayd) is by connection drawne from the
force and effect of faith, and to make it strong and good, I
said these two things must be added, þ faith needeth no outward helpe to minister matter of prayer, and that it can not
stande or be ioyned with any outward helpes, which I said
are both hereticall. He saith he will lay the wordes againe
before me, if peraduenture I may haue grace to call my
selfe backe. I looke vpon them againe, and although I did
not two yeares (as you vainely imagine) nor yet two daies,
consider of that one saying, yet can I not call my selfe back,
vnlesse

vnlesse I be conuinced with the light of truth: and that ye say I shalbe, and will so confirme your sayings by scriptures, that no peruerted spirit shalbe able to gainesay or resist. If the sighes and grones were of faith, that would minister matter without a booke, for the scripture (ye affirme) teacheth euerie where that in praying, the spirit onely helpeth our infirmities, no other helpes mentioned, or can be collected in the present action of praier through the scripture. He hath sét into our harts the spirit of his sonne crying Abba father, wee beleeue, therefore we speake. From hence now Maister Greenewood concludeth that I haue erred, and from an idle braine, & godles heart haue coined those heresies, because I constraine the proposition of the present action, in praying vnto a generall sentence of all times and actions. This is the summe of your answere, that before prayer there neede helpes and outward meanes, but in the present action of prayer, onely the spirit doth helpe, let vs see howe true this is, and how it dooth excuse yee from those hereticall opinions, which ye goe about to wipe away with this distinction.

First whereas yee say that in the verie time and action of prayer, it is the spirit alone without any outward means, because the scripture saith, God hath sent into our heartes the spirit of his sonne crying abba Father. I answere, that howsoeuer the scripture doth extoll or magnifie outwarde helpes, and meanes, yet when they are compared with God which worketh all in all by them, or when the scripture will set foorth the efficacie and worke to be his alone, they are either not mẽtioned, or else if they be mẽtioned, so cast down as if they were nothing. God buildeth his Church by the ministerie of men: yet he saith Paule planteth, Appollo watereth, but God giueth ẏ increase: So that neither he which plãteth is any thing, nor he that watreth, but God that giueth the increase. 1.Co.3. And therfore to gather frõ those sentences of scripture where the spirit of God is only mentioned to work praier, because the work is his alone, ẏ there neede or there may be no outward helps or meanes in the verie instant and action of praying, is farre awrie. For I would haue master Greenwood answere whether the voice of an other that prayeth, whether fasting, lifting vp the eyes and hands (which hee mentioned) or whether prostrating the bodie and kneeling be prayer it selfe, or outward meanes to make the prayer more feruent? Euerie simple man will laugh at him, if he say they be prayer it selfe, whereupon hee must bee forced to confesse they bee but outward helpes and meanes. Then aske master Greenwood againe, whether a man be to fast, to kneele downe, to prostrate his bodie, to lifte vp his eyes and hands onely before the action of prayer, or in praying? If he answere, what a question is that, what foole will say before: those things are to be done in the very instant and action of prayer. Then all men may see that master Greenwood hath brought this, I will not say from an idle braine, for I should not say true; but from an vnsound braine: that he may confirme by many testimonies of scripture, that the spirit onely helpeth our infirmities in the present action of prayer, that no peruerted spirit shalbe able to gayn-say or resist. Yee see the spirit of truth can resist it, and proue that not onely before prayer, but euen in the very action of prayer, outward helps and meanes especially for the ignorant and dull are needfull and good, and therefore the Brownists spirit is a false spirit, which saith, The scripture teacheth euery where that in praying the spirite onely helpeth our infirmities, no other helps mentioned or can be collected in the present action of praier. In the next place, where hee had said, A troubled heart is the pen of a readie writer, & therfore needeth not a booke. I sayd here can bee no good argument without an absolute perfection in knowledge, cheerefulnes, direction, memorie and vtterance, and that many are so perplexed in their troubles of heart, that they cannot pray, which through helpe of outward meanes doe powre foorth tears and supplications: He will not allow this for any answere; but doth distinguish of troubled mindes. The troubled minde he speaketh of, (which

which is the pen of a readie writer, is (when the minde is presently moued with the sight of some sin or vrged by other occasion,) a broken spirite, a broken and contrite heart. Psal. 51. and not the minde which in dispaire or doubt is perplexed. Then I answere that he must allow these latter the helpes and outward meanes, that they may be rid of their doubt and perplexitie. Moreouer, there is no man so perfect in faith, but he hath great remnants in him of dispaire and doubting. Why else did Dauid crie out, Correct me not in thy wrath, my bones are troubled. Psal. 6. Cast me not out from thy face Psal. 51 While I kept silence my bones did weare away, my moysture was turned into the drought in Summer. psal. 32. Hath God forgotté to be mercitul, hath he shut vp his compassiós in wrath, psal. 77. Whereupon it doth follow, that there is no man but may be sore troubled and perplexed with doubts, when the hand of God is heauie vpon him, and the sight of his sinnes doth terrifie him. It is not the glorie of faith to bee where there are no doubts of dispaire or no perplexities, but to get the victorie ouer them when they do assaile it. Therfore the ignoranter sorte in perplexitie need outward helps. The next part of mine answere, that such as be troubled and perplexed and cannot pray, are holpen by a booke, and by other meanes, hee doth allow and agree vnto, So that wee make reading one thing and praying another. Who doubteth that they be two things? did not I set downe at the first that the bodely action of reading is not the worship of God? Then master Greenwood hath his desire (seeing as he saith) wee cannot do both at once, he that prayeth speaketh to God, My God why doest thou hide thy face from me? But the Priest may say, My booke whie art thou so euill printed? For when they reade, the heart cannot reason aud talke with God. If the matter written in the booke bee a speach directed vnto God, as In thee O Lord haue I put my trust, let me neuer be confoũded, let master Greenewood or all the Brownists in the world, bring anie coulour of reason to prooue, that a man cannot at the same

 instant

instant both vtter it with his mouth in reading, and pray it with his heart. Master Greenwood must denie this againe. For alas what stuffe is this? or els how did they sing psalms to GOD and reade them vpon the booke? how can a man heare and pray both at one instant? Then in the next where he saith, I did but assume the question, in affirming that a man may pray by the spirit vpon a booke, &c. his argument being thus, That none worship God but they which from the inward faith of the heart bring foorth true inuocation. This doo not they that reade vpon the booke while they pray. I sayd he bringeth nothing to prooue the assumption, but that which is friuolous. For that it is sayd, wee would haue men in stead of powring foorth their hearts, to helpe themselues vpon a booke. I answere, that we wish men to vse the helpe of a booke that they may the better powre foorth their hearts to GOD, beeing such as are not otherwise throughly able. And that we would haue men to fetch the cause of their sighing and sorrowing from another mans writing, euen in the time of their begging at Gods hand. I answered, how fondlie doo ye make that to bee the cause, which doth but manifest the cause? For that which we reade or heare doth but shewe vnto vs the miserie which is within, and how it shall bee cured. Now let the reader obserue how simple shifts he findeth here. The first is the difference betweene reading and praying, the one beeing a powring foorth of supplications, the other a receiuing into the soule such things as wee reade. I pray ye tell me but this, when one heareth a prayer pronounced by another with whom he praieth, doth not his hearing receiue it into his soule, and at the very same instant also he doth powre it foorth as a praier to GOD? Are not the receiuing in and the powring foorth done both at once? How will he auoid the follie that I charged him withall, when receiuing in, and powring foorth, goe together at the samè instant? But it is beyond all the rest, that he saith, I graunt the whole question, by granting that reading the prayers is not the prayer, but an helpe. Is it all one to aske whether a man may be holpen to prayer by rea-

ding

ding, and whether the reading it selfe be praier? Hereupon hee also inferreth, that all our assemblies haue had none other inuocation of Gods name, but an helpe to teach them to power foorth their hearts. Then belike it followeth that wheresoeuer the helpe is, there is, or there can be no more: because such as read vpon a booke when they pray haue a good helpe to further them, therefore they doo not pray. Because I saide it is an helpe to such as bee not otherwise throughlie able: I must confesse that our whole Ministerie is vnable; a reason worthie a Brownist. There be other causes whie all Churches vse prescript forme, yea whereas all Ministers be able to pray without a booke.

Where I saide yee speake fondlie to call that the cause which dooth but manifest the cause: yee replie that I haue forgotten mine arts, because there be mo causes than one, there be instrumentall causes. I graunt there be moe causes than one. And it is certaine that the efficient cause is manifolde, if you meane by fetching the cause of their sorrowing from the booke in the time of their begging at Gods hand, the efficient cause instrumentall: I would haue yee but answer whether the instrumental cause cannot goe with the action, but the action is ouerthrowne or disgraced? I would also demaund whether it followe which yee collect, there is an instrumentall cause which is an helpe: therefore there is nothing else? Are these things other than trifles? I saide yee did answere nothing to that saying of our Sauiour, When ye pray, say our Father which art in Heauen, &c. Luke 11. Yee seeme, that yee will not answer vnles I conclude from this place by Syllogisme: but yet afterward yee doo. And indeede what needeth a Syllogisme where the words are of themselues sufficient, without anie further consequence or collection. If our Sauiour commaund to say those words praying, then is it most cleere, that to vse a prescript forme of words in praying is not idolatrie, nor a thing most detestable. But yee say yee manifested in your first writing, that our Sauiour did not commaund to vse those words when wee pray: but to pray according to

 that

that forme. Saint Matthew say you and Saint Luke, keep not the same words, nor that number of words: hee saide not reade these words, or say these words by roate when ye pray. These reasons I haue slilie passed ouer, as you accuse me. What reasons? If it be a reason there is but one: for Christs speech is plaine, when yee pray say thus: therefore we may vse those words. But must wee vse them of necessitie and neuer none other? Not so, but wee may vse, and it is necessarie for vs to vse particulars, which are conteined in those generals which are the ground and direction of all prayers. Your one reason or that which hath shew of reason is in this, that Saint Luke dooth omitte for thine is the Kingdome, &c. And that in the fourth and fift petitions they expresse the same matter with some difference of words. As though the question were about such a precisenes in words, that wee might not expresse the same petition in another phrase, but it ceaseth to be the same? Now where I conclude that it is therefore lawfull to vse a prescript forme of prayer, which is framed according to the Scriptures, in the assemblies. To this yee replie that because no mans writings are without error, it is pernicious and blasphemous doctrine which I collect. This yee affirme stoutlie, and for proofe bring nothing but those stale cauills which I haue sundrie times answered: and now yee will answer to the two places alleaged, Numb. 6. and Luke. 11. The priestes yee say were not commanded to vse those verie words of the blessing, when they blessed the people, the reason yee bring is from the Hebrew words which are as you say, Coh teborcu, thus shall yee blesse, Where the worde Coh is an aduerb of similitude, as we say after this manner: which cannot be to say the same, but according to the same instructions. This word Coh is vsed throughout the Bible in this manner, in all the prophets, when they say, thus saith the Lord. To this I answer, first let all men of anie meane learning, in the Hebrew bee witnes, how vnfit Master Greenewood is to reason from that tongue, when hee can not so much as reade two words of it aright. For he saicth

Coh

Coh teborcu, and it is Coh tebaracu. Then for the matter it selfe, this learned Hebrucian saith, that Coh being an aduerb of similitude, as we say after the same manner, it cannot be to say the same, but according to the same instructions. Where ignorance & boldnes are met together, what childre they bring forth ? We must beleeue that the Lord when he saith, thus shalt thou blesse, and prescribeth the words, willeth the Priests not to speake the same words, but the like. And when our Sauiour saith, When ye pray, say thus, Our father &c. It is as much as if he should say, in any wise say not these wordes at any time, but the like. For, thus, is not the same, but the like. God sayd to Moses, I will send thee to Pharao, that thou maiest bring the children of Israel out of Egypt. Moses draweth backe, saying, when I shall come to the children of Israel and shall say vnto them, the God of your fathers hath sent me vnto ye: If they shall say vnto me, what is his name? what shall I say vnto them? The Lord sayd, Thus shalt thou say to the children of Israel, Eheie hath sent me vnto ye. Moreouer, God sayd to Moses, Thus shalt thou say vnto them, The God of your fathers, the God of Abraham, the God of Isaak, the God of Iaacob hath sent me vnto ye. Exod. 3. vers. 13, 14, 15.

Now, according to Master Greenwoods exposition of Coh, Moses is not commanded to say those words but the like. If they should demaund what is his name that hath sent thee: he may not say Eheie hath sent me, because God sayd Coh, that is thus, which is not the same words but the like. He might not say the God of Abraham, the God of Isaak, the God of Iaacob hath sent me vnto ye, which GOD saith is his name and memoriall for euer, because God sayd Coh, that is, thus shalt thou say, but hee must say the like words. He saith further, that Coh is so vsed in all the Prophets, when it is sayd, thus saith the Lord. That is, GOD hath not spoken these very words, which wee bring, might the Prophets say, but the like. It is a like thing that Master Greenwood, or some other Hebrucian among the Brownists, hath read ouer al the Prophets in the Hebrew tongue, to knowe how Coh is euerie where vsed, when he could not reade two wordes right. And now what shall we say of the Scriptures? the wordes, if wee shall beléeue the Brownists, are not Gods wordes, but the wordes of the Prophets. Is this wholesome doctrine? Did the Prophets bring any one word which GOD did not put into their mouth? I pray ye Master Greenwood, or any other Brownist, tell me, did not God speake in the Prophets all the wordes that they vttered, euen at the verie instant when they say, thus saith the Lord? How can it then so wickedly be sayd, they were not the very same wordes which God spake, but the like, because the aduerb thus doth signifie the like, and not the same? But hée rendreth a reason, which is, that we haue but the summe of their prophesies recorded vnto vs by the holie Ghost, and not all the words. Because we haue not all the wordes, therefore haue we not the same in those that are set downe? Did the holie Ghost vse this word Coh, to giue vs to vnderstand that there is written but an abridgement or summe of matters, and not the same wordes, that they were vttered in, but some such like? Againe, did the holie Ghost recorde them, & are they not all his wordes which are written in the summe of the prophesies set downe? Shall we beléeue this man? I doo beléeue him in this that he saith the holie Ghost did recorde them: for therein he speaketh the trueth. But when he saith, that thus saith the Lord, is not these same wordes saith the Lord, but the like, because thus is an aduerb of likenes, it is a vile saying. Is not the holie Ghost the Lord? If hée had spoken those things before in moe wordes, and now recordeth them in fewer, saying, thus saith the Lord, doth not he speake these fewer wordes which are written, as well as those moe wordes which were vttered? Are they not then, thus saith the Lord, euen the verie same wordes which the Lord speaketh, and not like? If ye make many such expositions of wordes ye may leade me whether ye will. There is then another reason rendred to proue that the Priests were not tied vnto those wordes in blessing the people, namely, that in prayer they are blessed in the Psalmes and in the

Chro-

Chronicles with many other words. And Eli bleſſed Hanna in other words. It is not the queſtion whether at any time the people might bee bleſſed in other words, in fewer, or in moe: but whether the Prieſts had not that forme preſcribed to vtter in bleſſing the whole aſſemblie, and whether it were Idolatrie to vſe thoſe preſcript phraſes of wordes? As likewiſe it is not maintained that when our Sauiour ſaith, ſay thus, that wee may not pray in other words, or expreſſe our petitions more particularlie: but that we may vſe thoſe words and ſentences as moſt excellent petitions. Againſt this Maſter Greenwood bringeth nothing in his words that followe. For Maſter Caluine neuer held it vnlawful to pray in that forme of words, though he teach truelie, that men are not ſo tied vnto it, that they may vſe none other. And therefore it ſtandeth firme and ſure that the forme of words in the Lords Prayer is to bee lawfullie vſed praying.

In the next part Maſter Greenwood is in a great heate, and maketh an outcrie to call men to the beholding of an iniurie, which I, as he ſaith, as a godles man haue done him. Here (ſaith he) I muſt call all men that reade this fruitles diſcourſe, to be witneſſe, &c. Indeede ye may well call it a fruitles diſcourſe, which ye call men that reade to beare witneſſe with ye: and let the reader iudge by your expoſition of Coh, whether it be not worſe than fruitleſſe which ye ſpread among the ignorant ſort, which are readie to ſucke in ſuch filthie dregges. The abuſe of my tongue to the defacing of Gods trueth, is that I ſayd, he calleth all men Idolaters. And to make the matter cléere that he ſpake not the words, but I my ſelfe, he maketh a briefe repetition how we fell into that matter. But before we procéede any further, I pray ye tell me what is the reaſon, that I hauing ſet downe your whole diſcourſe touching this poynt, ſo that you cannot denie but that I haue alſo ſet it downe truely, you forſake that and ſet downe vp péece meale but ſome of your words, and reaſon from them: If I had ment in a godles manner wilfully to peruert your words, would I haue deliuered them whole and together in print: It seemeth ye haue some hope that some men will reade your booke, which will not compare it with mine, or which being carried with blind heate, cannot. Now I craue no more of the reader but to marke the whole speach which you deliuered, and mine answere to it, and to iudge indifferently. If Master Greenwoods words bee not such as must needes include that which I haue collected, let me beare the blame for that matter, which is one of the least. He saith I haue an euasion to auoide this foyle, because I sayd I tooke it we reasoned about such grosse Idolatrie, as a Church is to bee condemned and forsaken for which is defiled therewith. He saith he neuer reasoned to that end in this whole discourse. And I say then he must go from his owne words, which affirme that read prayer offered vp to GOD as a sacrifice is Idolatrie: that to reade the prayer while one praieth, is a chaunging the worke of the spirit into an Idoll, a bondage and breaking of Christian libertie, a thing most detestable, a deuice of Antichrist. Let all men iudge by these speaches what manner of Idolatrie was in question betweene vs. Master Greenwood as if he had wonne the field, will needs put me to my raunsome, and asketh what mends I will make him for this slandering? I answer, that as your victorie is but in a dreame, so my raunsome must be therafter. If I could see I had done ye wrong, I would be sorie. He will haue no man free from such foule Idolatrie, but yet no Idolaters. No Church is free ye confesse from all spot vpon earth. Hereupon ye growe againe into a newe heate, and charge me out of one mouth to giue contrarie sentence, because I call ye Donatists. Why man, are ye ignorant of this, that the Donatists did confesse all men to bee sinners, and yet the arguments by which they would maintaine their schisme could not bee strong, vnlesse they would maintaine a perfection, and some of their reasons though they ment not so reached so farre. And so is it with you Brownists. If one should followe ye in all the grosse absurdities which will followe from your exposition of Coh, thus saith the Lord, could you haue any way but to

protest

protest ye did meane no such thing? Wee may not looke what men protest they hold, but what doth followe of their reasons, and then ye shall see that such as be in schisme and heresie are with the blasts of their swelling pride toised and hurled vpon contrarie Rockes. Now, whereas I sayd the confession of the Brownists, that there is no Church in earth without spottes of Idolatrie, doth ouerthrowe the reasons which they bring to condemne the Church of England. Because they cannot argue thus, this is a fault, it is Idolatrie: therefore this or that assemblie which is spotted is no true Church. But they must proue the Idolatrie to bee such as destroyeth the faith, &c. Master Greenwood would beare men in hand, that I reason as simplie, as to say, if there bée no true Church in earth without spots, then the Church of Rome is the true Church, for that hath many spots. I answere, that we doo not take it that the spots doo make it a true Church, but because there bee onely spottes and not fundamentall errors? The foolish cauill here is that I assume that which I should proue. Doo I not prooue it by answering the vile and shameles slaunders of yours, when ye affirme euerie spot in our Churches to be blasphemies and heresies and abominations, and Egyptian sores? You must prooue these your slaunders true, and I will cease.

Now we come to the arguments which were set down at the first. No Apocrypha is to be brought into the publike assemblies, all read prayer is Apocripha. Here you say I haue nothing to vtter, and yet oppose against both propositions, to royle the doctrine with my feete least others should drink of it. I sayd your proposition is false because the exposition of the scriptures by the preacher, and the prayers of the preacher are not canonicall, which your proposition doth exclude. Your replie is, that the Sermons and prayers of of the Preacher be the liuely voyce of Gods owne graces which ye mention in your proposition, and so neither Canonicall, nor Apocripha: and so not excluded. Touching the Paraphrase vpon the Psalmes in meeter, I holde not Canonicall in some respects: If you banish all writings that be

 not

not Canonicall, then ye banish then. Your answere is, that if I will affirme them to be Apocrypha, as ye say I cannot but doe; you will proove they are not to be brought into the publike assemblies. Your proofes doe follow: First no mans writings are giuen by the testimonie of Gods spirit, whome alone we are to heare. No mans writings are without errors and imperfections: The Church is builded vpon the foundation of the Apostles and Prophets: If we might bring in mens writings, then al mens writings which are agreeable to Gods word. No mans writings carie that maiestie that the pen of the holy ghost. No mans writings are authentike confirmed by signes and wonders. The scripture is all sufficient; al men must walk by that one rule: To think there were not rules enough prescribed by the Lorde for his house, is blasphemous and papisticall. Then ye say, the gifts to prophesie, are not Apocryphall, and so ye conclude your proposition: that onely Gods word and the liuely graces of his holy spirite are to be offered vp vnto him in the publike assemblies. Then touching your assumption: I sayd I see not how our speech to God should be called Apocrypha. Ye replie y^t it answereth not you, which do not holde an other mans writing to be our speech vnto God. Finally because I said that Apocrypha is that which is not Gods vndoubted worde vnto vs: yee say I haue ouerthrowen my selfe and cast out all read prayer, in as much as I deny them to be Canonicall. And so affirming that I haue not in both writings made one direct answer to this most firme proposition: Onely the Canonicall scriptures and liuely voice of Gods own graces are to be brought into the publike assemblies for doctrine and prayers: But mens writings are neither Canonicall, nor the liuely voice of Gods owne graces. Now master Greenwood hauing thus played the man in erecting (as he supposeth) so mighty a piller, that cannot be shaken, could content himselfe to go no further. I might end here saith hee with this vaine man, considering the whole matter is proued against him: And all that followeth but repetitions of the same cauills; but that I must cleare

my

my selfe of his vneoncionable slaunders. Hee triumphing thus fully, what shall I doe now? I aunswere, first that hee is much deceiued and would deceiue others: as it is written, The deceiuers shall wax worse and worse, deceiuing and being deceiued. For like as one that among many Apples doth hide and sell one Crab, so he among many true principles doth bring in one false conclusion which deceiueth his Schollers. For if he did reason thus, wee must heare onely the voice of Gods spirite, therefore all things in the Church are to be tried by the voice of the spirit. No mans writings are without errors and imperfections: therefore mē cannot ground vpon them any further than they be consonant to the Canonicall scriptures. The Church is builded vpon the foundation of the Apostles and Prophets, therfore our faith is to rest no further vpon the sayings and writings of men, than they be prooued by the doctrine of the Apostles & Prophets; he should conclude a truth which is vnanswerable. But now where master Greenwoods conclusiō is after this sorte, therefore nothing but the Canonicall scriptures, and the liuely voice of Gods graces is to bee brought into the publike assemblies; he concludeth falsely, as shall appeare. For if nothing but the perfect rule it selfe is to bee brought into the Church: If nothing done by man which hath errors in it, is to haue place in the assemblies: If nothing but eyther such or that which is the liuely voyce of Gods owne graces is to be vttered in the congregation; then must bee cast foorth not onely al written prayers: but also ẏ whole bible, vnles it be in ẏ Hebrew & Greeke, with the Sermons and praiers of the Pastors. For there is no translation of the Bible without errors, and the bookes are thus farre mans writing respecting onely the translation. And furthermore we decide not controuersies by any translation of the Bible, but by the authentike copies of the Hebrew and Greek, in one of which the olde testament is set downe by the Prophets, in the other the new testamēt by the Apostles. So that your conclusion doth not shut out onely the Psalmes in meeter, but the whole scriptures; vnles you will be so bolde as to say that translations be without errors, and so the perfect rule.

And now touching the second part, will Master Greenwood bee so vnwise as to affirme that the errours in the Sermons and in the prayers of the Pastors, bee the liuely voyce of Gods owne graces? He will assuredly denie it: for the graces of G O D (all simple men know) bring not foorth errors. Then let him marke his conclusion, no mens writings are without errours and imperfections, therefore no mens writings are to be brought into the publike assemblie: is not this conclusion as strong, no translations of the Bible, no Psalmes in meeter, no Sermons, nor Prayers of the Pastors, are without errors and imperfections, therfore none of these are to be brought into the publike assemblies? Is there any so voide of sense, that can not tast howe sower this Crabbe is, which Maister Greenewood conueieth in among so many sweete Apples? But he replieth further to confirme his matter by argument thus, if anie mens writings may bee brought into the publike assemblies, then al mens writings which are thought to be agreeable to Gods word, may be brought in. To prooue the consequence of this proposition, he saith; If God commaunde any to be brought in as being agreeable to the Scriptures, then by that commaundement all are to bee brought in that be agreeable: If there be no commandement, then none are to be brought in. I answere that God hath commaunded that in the Church all thinges bee done for edification, now the prayers being the same, being holy & good, are of like maiestie & dignitie in thẽselues vttered by him that conceaueth them, or from a prescript forme, the matter resteth not in that, but in the faith and feruencie of those that pray, there be errours and imperfections, as well in the one as in the other, but to auoide inconuenience, and for the benefite of the simpler sort, a prescript forme is needefull, & so farre commaunded. Then see how friuolous this conclusion is, that so all mens writinges which are thought to be agreeable to the word, are to bee brought in, seeing

seeing that which is conuenient in some, is not conuenient in all. His reasons which follow are in effect all one with the former, and proue not that conclusion of his, to shut forth the prescript forme of prayer. Let the Brownist now set the word Apocripha aside, which is but a woord, and not of the Scriptures, and go to the matter it selfe, drawing by firme conclusion that nothing is to be allowed any place in the Church which is not the perfect rule it selfe, in writing, or without errours vttred in speech, and I will yeelde. But this shall all the Brownistes in the world be neuer able to do, as I haue sufficiently shewed before. What then, or where is his glorie and victorie which he boasteth off, to be such that hee needeth to proceede no further? But nowe I woulde haue the reader to vnderstande my meaning aright, and how I argue: least any should thinke I compare the hauing the Bible in a translation, and the prayers and Sermons of the Pastors, with the prescribed forme of prayer, to be of but equall or like necessitie. The summe of that I set downe is to this effect, that it is false which Maister Greenewood standeth to prooue, namely that nothing with errour in it is to bee brought into the publicke assemblies, seeing there is a necessitie of hauing the scriptures in a translation: there is also a necessitie of hauing the sermons and Prayers of the Ministers, and yet errours in both, that which is of necessitie to be had, may not bee cast foorth, because of imperfections and errours: then also prescript forme of prayers, though not of necessitie, yet for conuenientcie vnto edification, is not to be cast foorth, because of imperfections, being not to increase, but to diminish the errours in praying.

The next argument is this, Wee must doe nothing in the worship of God, without warrant of his word. Read prayers haue no warrant of his woorde.

How false this assumption is, namely, That to reade a prayer when one doth pray, or to followe a prescript forme, hath no warrant in Gods woord, I haue shewed by by sundrie scriptures and reasons, and answered al the shifts brought against them, for which I referre the Reader to my former booke.

Maister Greenewood pressed with the waight of truth, and finding he had vttred grosse matter, could be content (but that as he saith to answere vnconscionable slaunders) to stay in the first argument : as hauing wonne the field, but yet he goeth on, and by vaine shiftes wil doe as well as he can to couer his fault. First he accuseth me that not hauing answered one reason, I haue with much euill conscience (as the handling sheweth) peruerted them, saying hee will leaue them to be iudged of them that shall see his writing : and seeing I would not Print it, he will answere my chief obiections. Touching this I answere, that your words are manie, and I esteemed it a wearisome matter to write them all, accounting it sufficient to note your reasons, but looke what so euer ye complayne off, that I haue peruerted and done ye wrong in, ye shall haue them in those pointes fully and wholy deliuered, that all the worlde may see and iudge betweene vs, whether I haue wilfully, and vnconscionably, and as a godlesse man (as ye accuse me) charged ye with any one thing which your words doe not containe.

Now to proceede to your replie : First, yee say that I graunt your Argument is sounde, if yee put difference between reading vpon the booke, and that which one hath learned out of the booke. For by your owne confession (say you) God hath not giuen any commandement to read prayer, and so it hath no warrant. Hereupon yee charge mee, that as an vnconstant man, I call back againe that which I had graunted: I saide I did not remember that euer I did read in the holie Scriptures that God commandeth the prayer shall bee read vpon the Booke, If I haue called now to remembrance, where it is reade, It were no vnconstancie to say now, there is commaundement. But in deede I doe not remember I haue euer reade any such commaundement. But now you boast of your gaines by this confession, saying that I graunt then there is no warrant. Lay all my words together

together, and yee may put your gaine in your eye, and see neuer the worse. I set downe first of all that it is great audacitie, to affirme that there is no warrant of the word, for read prayer, seeing there be sundrie testimonies to warrant the same, as I haue shewed: for the Lord prescribed a forme of blessing, and commaunded the Priests so to blesse Num. 6. He prescribed a forme of prayer for the people at the offering the first fruites, and cōmaunded thē to vse it Deutr. 26 The Psalme for the sabaoth was commaunded to bee song, the Psalme 22. was to bee song euerie morning, and these they were tied vnto by expresse commaundement, though not to the booke, because it is more commendable to haue them by heart. And the Lorde dooth not tye a man to that which is lesse cōmendable. This is the summe of that reason which I vsed, from whence there is warrant to followe a prescript forme. Master Greenewood vrgeth this, if there be no commaundement, then there is no warrant: and affirmeth it to bee inconstancie to say there is no commaundement to reade praying, and yet some warrant for it by the word. I haue answered, that God tied the Priests and people vnto some prescript formes, though not precisely to the booke. And though that were legall, and no such commaundement to tie men of necessitie: now yet it sheweth the thing to be holie and lawfull. Further I adde, if wee respect the matter as we say in the These, or for a generalty there is no commandement: for then it should bee of necessitie and not for conueniencie. But if we regarde it in the Hypothese for circumstances in particularitie, there is commaundement: as thus, God hath commaunded those thinges too bee done which serue as helpes for edification, or be most conuenient. Then where the state of anie man, or the state of the assemblies is such, as that prescript forme of prayer is conuenient and needefull for edification, there it is commanded. Now let the reader obserue againe your words, which are that al our ministers must leaue reading their stinted praiers vpon the booke, or else stand vnder Gods wrath, and all that so praye with them. Master Greenewood complaineth of great iniury, whē I gather from his words, that he condemneth all Churches, because hee knoweth that is a matter sufficient alone to bewray the wickednes of Brownisme. Now if all our Ministers which pray vpon the booke, and the people, that pray with them stand vnder the wrath of God for this thing, then cannot they be the Church of God: for GOD loueth his Church; and all Churches haue prescript formes of prayer which their Ministers vse: therfore they all stand vnder Gods wrath. But they doo it ignorantlie, will he say; and so (say I) did all our Churches, vntill his papers came abroad, and manie haue not as yet seene them: and some that haue seene them are not perswaded, and so are ignorant still. The next thing ye deale with, is the Argument which I drawe from the singing Psalmes vpon the booke: it is so cleere they did sing them vpon the booke, that the Brownist himselfe cannot denie it. It is also most manifest they did sing them (as hee also now confesseth) to God, for so are we commaunded in many places, sing praises to God. Then further he that offereth vp praise to God reading, it cannot be gainsaide, but that he offereth vp a spirituall sacrifice to God reading. Yea praise is one parte of prayer: and it is as hard a thing to speake praises to God vpon the booke, as to craue by petitions vpon the booke, and as spirituall a worke; and I may say a more high seruice: where is then that grosse fantasie of Master Greenewood, which because reading is one thing; and speaking to God is another, saith a man cannot both read and speake to God at once. He cannot say O my God when he readeth, but O my booke why art thou so euill printed? I argue if the people of God in olde time, did both reade the Psalmes vpon the booke, and speake vnto the Lord at the same instant: how should it not now bee both possible and lawfull, for to speake vnto God in praiers while one readeth? Hee saieth, I denie your Argument. I say that is not sufficient to denie the Argument: let vs therefore see the reasons of the deniall. Admitte that singing were a part of praier (sayeth he) yet dooth it not follow that all praier may bee read vpon

the

the booke: we must take this vpon your bare word, at least such as will, may beléeue yee. I stand to affirme that one part of praier is as spirituall a worke as another; thereupon I also affirme, that if one part may bee read vppon the booke, and no turning the worke of the spirite into an Idoll, no stinting the spirite, no quenching the spirit, no Idolatrie, no hindrance, but that hee which readeth may speake vnto God: it may be so in any other part. And let vs see what hee will bee able to disproue this withall? But hee saieth I speake like an ignorant man, to say that singing is praier, because they be two diuers actions and exercises of our faith. The one neuer read for the other, nor saide to be a parte of the other, throughout the Scriptures, but are plainelie distinguished, As I will praye with the Spirite, I will pray with vnderstanding, I will sing with the spirit, I will sing with vnderstanding, saith Saint Paul. I answer you could no where more vntimelie accuse mee of ignorance, then where your owne speech in this and that which followeth next, is patched vp with errors, almost as thick as the patches vpon a beggars cloake. And for answere I say, first, that Saint Paul doth distinguish them there is great reason, not onelie because the verie singing it selfe is not praier, no more then reading or speaking: but also that there bee manie praiers which are not song, and manie Psalmes and songs, which are no formes of praier; nor the spéech directed to God: a prayer that is no psalme is neuer called a psalme, nor any reason why it should: but a Psalme that is a praier, is called both a Psalme and a praier. The Psalme 86. is called Tephillah a praier, and consisteth of sundrie petitions. The Psalme 90. is so called, being the praier of Moses. Psalme 102. is called Tephillah leaani, the praier for the poore, when hee is in perplexitie, and powreth forth his meditatiō before the Lord. The people praying for Christs Kingdome did vse to say, Hosanna, Blessed is he that commeth in the name of the Lord. Psal. 118. The Psalme 50. and 119. with many other containe petitions, almost in euery verse, which if a man did pray or desire them earnestly

 singing,

singing, it was no Idolatrie: singing I graunt is not called praier, but men might sing Psalmes to God, and were commanded, which contained praises and petitions: but they were giuen to the Church, to be song or read in ÿ forme of praier (saith he) but denieth ÿ this was to be done praying. He not only confesseth they were to sing thē vnto God, but also saith the Lord keep me frō such an error, as to denie that: & yet euē in this cōfession falleth into as grose a matter. for what can bee more absurd, than that a man should vtter and speake euen vnto God that which is a prayer and yet might not pray: as when out of the Psalm. 118. praying for the kingdome of Christ, they cried Hosanna, blessed is he that commeth in the name of the Lord: or when for some speciall benefite the whole Church was to sing prayse to God, and had a prescript forme deliuered vnto them: were they to mocke with God, and not to speak prayses vnto him indeede from the heart and with chearefulnes: or did God commaund them to doe two things which cannot bee done at once: or wil any deny that many in singing, (though the singing it selfe be not praying) doe giue hearty thankes to God where thanksgiuing is expressed, and craue earnestly when they vtter petitions: Master Greenewood doth grieuously complaine of me for doing him foule wrong in saying he denieth that the Psalmes are to be sung to God. And what other thing in effect doth he vtter here, when hee saith they were not to vtter the wordes of a Psalme to God praying? But I will set downe his first words which are these. The same may be sayde for the hundreth and second Psalme: for although some haue taken it as a prayer of the Prophet when he was in affliction, yet may I graunt with you to be taken in the future tense, and auoyd that superstition you would fall into, for if it had beene giuen vnto the Church to haue beene read as a prayer vnto God, it should haue beene saide, O Lord heare our prayer, and let our crie come vnto thee. And therefore it is manifest that this Psalme was giuen to the Isralites in time of their captiuitie at Babylon, or some other such calamitie, to comfort

fort and instruct them how to settle themselues, and powre foorth their prayers before the Lord. But howe will you prooue that the people were to say ouer these wordes vnto God? for wee may see the like by Habbacuc, prescribing the people a forme of prayers to comfort themselues, and deliuered it to be sung in the assemblies. Moreouer after manie other wordes master Greenwood sayth thus: And that singing of Psalmes is no part of prayer we may see by the exhortation which the Apostle vseth to the Ephesians, saying Speake vnto your selues in Psalmes and Hymnes and spirituall songs: And to the Collos. where it is sayde Let the word of God dwel in ye plenteously in al wisdome teaching & admonishing your selues in psalmes & hymnes and spiritual songs. And further we reade that Christ our Sauiour did giue thanks and then sing a Psalme after the institution of the Lords Supper: for that singing is a reioysing our selues, and instructing our selues.

Now let the reader iudge, by comparing that which I haue written in my former booke with these words of his, whether I or he be the godles man which dealeth by vnconscionable slaunders, and with much euil conscience. Master Greenwood denying the vse of prescript forme when wee speake vnto God, and I alleadging the Psalmes, demandeth how I wil proue that the people were to say ouer those wordes vnto God? And after as you see to prooue that the wordes were not to be vttered or said ouer to God praying, he alleageth the sayings of Paule, Speaking to your selues and instructing your selues in Psalmes and Hymnes and spirituall songs, leauing out in both places the latter ende of the sentence of singing to the Lord. Now when I haue proued that the verie wordes of some Psalmes were to be said ouer to God, because the scripture is cleare in many places, Sing Psalmes to God, sing praysesto God, &c. and charged him with denying that the Psalmes are to be sung to God contrarie to such expresse commandement, and blamed him for leauing out the parte of the sentence which maketh against him, he crieth shame vpon me. But master Green-

wood

wood it is the light of Gods word, and the waight thereof which doth presse ye, and cutteth downe all vngodly fantasies, and not I. You confesse now, because the scripture is plaine, that the Psalmes were to be sung to God, and yet ye did aske how I would prooue the people were to say ouer the words. Then it followeth that the verie prescript forms of wordes were to be saide ouer to God by your confession, which is the whole matter that I haue stoode to prooue. And now chuse whether you will denie that Psalmes were to be sung to God, or confesse that those verie wordes of the Psalmes and the prescript formes were to be said ouer vnto him in singing.

What will he say now? This he will say, that they were in those words to be song vnto God, but not praying: for he saith I must proue the Church did vse to reade the psalmes for praying, I wonder how a man can speake to God the sentences which are praiers, and not praying. Againe I would haue any Brownist shew mee what speach wee can haue to God which is not praier: if he say a man dooth speak to God in giuing him thankes and praise, in acknowleging his benefites, in ascribing vnto him all wisdome, power, glorie, goodnes, bountifulnes, faithfulnes, and mercie. A man dooth speake to God, when hee confesseth his sinnes, when he complaineth of the iniuries and wrongs of others: I confesse, and I say withall, that they be all of them parts of praier. Why dooth a man giue thankes and praise, and mention Gods benefits; but to support his faith, and hope that he shall receiue further, and to moue the Lord to continue still good vnto him, or such like? Why doo we speake vnto him of his glorious power, wisdome, mercie and trueth, but that our faith and praier dooth rest vpon those pillers? Why doo we confesse our sinnes, but as intreating for pardon; and what doo we rehearse the vniust outrage of our aduersaries, but to procure his iust defence and protection? But hee demandeth what this maketh for reading praiers framed by men? I answer to the same effect which I haue euer done, that this is one of the porest cauilles that may

bee

be among a thousand. We reason not about the matter of praiers, but about the reading: for if the matter bee corrupt and naught, the pronouncing or the reading cannot make it better. If the matter be erronious, it is no more authentick pronounced, then read: if it be pure and good pronounced, the reading cannot hurt it, or make it unpure. The reading it selfe is not unpure when we speake to God: for then should not the Psalmes haue been song upon the booke unto him. Who is so senceles then as not to see this conclusion to follow, to utter a prescript forme of words, in a Psalme when one speaketh to God is no sinne. Therefore to followe a prescript forme of words in any godly praier, when one praieth is not sinne; for where shall we finde the sinne? If it be in following a prescript forme, it should haue been unlawfull to followe it in the Psalmes. If it be in the matter, because there bee errors in all mens writings; and therefore to bee cast forth: then I say the errors, and not the reading is in the fault, and for which only there must be the casting forth, and so we must cast forth the praiers of the preachers. To his next words, I answer that it is not the repeating ouer the same godlie petitions againe euery day, that maketh it the sacrifice of fooles, but when men doo it of custome without faith and feruent affection: for if a man with faith and zeale pray euery day the same praier to God, it is acceptable. The rest of his words are not worth the repeating, and yet he concludeth most falsly that read praier hath no warrant in Gods word.

The next Argument is this, We may not in the worship of God receiue any tradition, which bringeth our libertie into bondage: read praier vpon commandement is a tradition that dooth bring our libertie into bondage.

Against this I opposed that Moses, the Prophets, and our Sauiour gaue prescript formes of praiers, and if the very following a prescript forme imposed by commandement, be so detestable a thing, how are not they charged with this heinous sinne? He answereth that here is a great storme, and yet nothing but winde; doo ye not know the wind may

bee

be so great, as to blow downe the house vpon your head, especially when the blast of truth commeth against your building, which standeth vpon the rotten pillers of errours. The counterfaite zeale of Cayphas against the trueth, ought not to stay any man from being earnest for the truth. But now to the matter, your woonted song was heretofore when such prescript formes were alleadged, proue that those wordes were to be saide ouer to God: but now being conuinced, and confessing that some Psalmes were song to God, and for feare least bidding mee prooue againe that the prescript forme was followed, when they spake to GOD, I should againe charge ye openly to denie the singing of Psalmes to God, which I haue shewed yee doe couertly, ye seeke another shift, and say your Minor proposition (which is that I stand to disprooue) speaketh of the reading for praying, and not of the forme of prayer. This is poore stuffe, seeing we reason about prescript forme and reading the same, praying. I do not say that the reading it selfe is praying: but I haue prooued, that they went together, and whether there were cōmandement to followe the prescript formes or not, in the blessing, for the Priestes to vse. In the prayer prescribed for the people to say at the offring the first fruites, and in some of the Psalmes, whether it be not also lawful to say the Lords prayer praying, let wise men iudge. Nowe where as I saide the Brownistes doe condemne all Churches by these three arguments against read prayers, Maister Greenewood at this is in no small heate as his speech doth shewe: for if hee coulde dippe his wordes tenne times deeper in gall, it appeareth hee woulde not spare. I trust (saith he) your madnesse will appeare vnto all men, the poyson of Aspes is vnder your tongue. But Maister Greenewood, If I haue saide the truth which is iustifiable by your owne speeches, your sober minde is not to bee boasted off. And if your sentence include all Churches, what milke and honie doth flow from vnder your lippes? Heere is much a doe, this man layeth about him as if he were halfe madde: but that he is blindfolde, I could not escape some

sounde

sounde blowes. Here he hath vp the begger with his clappe dish, and the Priest with his Masse booke, sanuesing ouer the Pater noster for their bellie. Here he saith I breath out my accustomed lies, slaunders, and raylings, calling them Brownists and Donatists, here he detesteth Donatus his heresies: Browne, and the Brownists, he saith are ours, hee willeth mee to remember who is the Father of such vntruthes, when I say they condemne al reformed Churches, but because my conscience (as hee saith) did witnesse I had wrongfullie charged him, and for him all true Christians, I bring it in by necessarie consequence. Now if the heate be any thing past heare a little what I saye, shewe that I haue any way slaundred ye, or rayled vpon yee, in that I haue termed you Brownists and Donatists: and let mee haue open shame among all men. I haue affirmed that the very pith of all your matter is from Maister Brownes bookes, conuince mee therein if yee can, I haue now published that Brownisme and Donatisme are all one: let any Brownist in the land confute me. The theefe will not abide to be so called, but will say I defie all theeues: doth that cleare him when he liueth by theeuerie? what are you the better to say I detest the heresies of Donatus, and yet holde all that he helde, and know not what ye say, nor what the heresies of Donatus were, more then doth a post: shew openly that ye renounce those thinges I haue noted to bee the furies of the Donatists, & then yee may crie out that ye are slaundred.

And now for condemning al Churches, will ye denie that which is concluded by necessarie consequence from your words? Is that against conscience which is brought in by necessarie consequence? Ye would seeme to make light of it in this respect, that a multitude is not to bee followed to doo euill, when ye condemne all Churches: but yet it doth sting ye so neere, that by no meanes ye can abide to heare of it. Thus I did reason, and thus I reason still without any witnesse of conscience against me. You affirme prescript formes of prayer brought into the publike assemblies, to bee

the changing the worke of the spirit into an Idoll, a tradition breaking Christian libertie, and therefore a thing most
detestable, a dead letter which doth quench the spirit; but
all reformed Churches haue prescript forme of prayer imposed: therefore yee condemne all Churches. I am glad
your booke may bee seene of all men, that they may iudge
the soundnes of that answere by which ye would cleere your
selfe. Ye cannot goe from your first words, they be spread
in the hands of so many, but ye should shame your selfe. Ye
replie therefore againe, that the true Churches might erre
in this, and yet remaine Churches of God. This is strange
that ignorance should excuse men that worship an Idoll in
stead of God, that take away the Christian libertie from the
consciences of men, and doo that which is most detestable.
What doo the Papists more than these? or what can they
bee charged withall which is worse than that which is most
detestable? And haue ye not set downe now in this your
booke in replying vpon the second Argument, that all our
Ministers must leaue reading their stinted prayers, or else
stand vnder Gods wrath and all that pray with them? How
are the Ministers and people of other Churches priuiledged
from standing vnder Gods wrath, hauing read prayers, imposed leiturgies, and as you terme them stinted prayers? or
tell me, are they the Churches of God that stand vnder his
wrath? Now remember who is the father of lyes. Well,
your meaning was not to condemne the Churches, nor to
meddle with them. Why then doo ye giue such sentence of
condemnation which reacheth vnto them? Tel me but this,
is there any Brownist which is a disciple, and giueth credite
vnto ye in this matter, that read prayer is most detestable,
and that such as ioyne in it stand vnder Gods wrath, which
yet durst ioyne himselfe or might ioyne himselfe vnto any
assemblie in the world, euen the most reformed? Tell me either you or any other chiefe Brownist, will say they may
pray with any assembly where they follow a prescript forme?
If ye dare not say this (I meane that ye would counsell men
to ioyne with a Church that hath read prayer) but say they
must

must reproue and condemne it, and if it were not redressed forsake them: then bee also ashamed so furiouslie to crie out vpon me, which speake nothing herein, that I say ye condemne all churches, but that which all indifferent men must néedes sée your owne wordes and doctrine doe vpholde. As for your bitter accusations vpon no shewe I leaue them: and whereas ye require that if I haue any sparkle of grace, I would procure that ye might decide the trueth with other Churches. I answere, that if ye had any sparke of sober wisdome, ye could not with such condition lay that vpon me, which ye knowe not howe vnable I am to performe. You say you might iustly be called an Anabaptist, if you should reason thus, Imposing of mens writings to be read for praying, is an heinous sinne, therefore they that vse it are no Church. Haue ye said no more, but that it is an hainous sinne? Haue you forgotten all your former sayings of Idolatrie, bondage breaking Christian libertie, most detestable, standing vnder Gods wrath? I hold him no Anabaptist nor Donatist, which from such spéeches concludeth no true Church. For I neuer heard that the true Church doth stand vnder Gods wrath. The next wordes are sore; Abaddon is the father of such Prophets, saith Maister Greenewood, because I say the Brownists maintaine such a fréedome as that will haue nothing imposed by commaundement. I pray ye tell me whether you be one of those which set out the brief summe of the profession? And when I had written against it, I would knowe if ye were one that made the defence, or approued the same? Did yee not approue of the answers that goe vnder the name of Henrie Barrow? Imposed is put for an argument by it selfe in those writings, and so noted with a figure. Could the very word imposed be an argument by it selfe, if any imposing by commaundement bee lawfull in Gods worship? If the ciuill Magistrates haue power but to reuiew the lawes of Christ, and to moue men or stirre them vp to the more diligent keeping of the same, may they then impose by commaundement? And as you speake here of that which is not onely receiued, but also by

 com-

commaundement, as though there were great waight in the words, by commaundement. I pray ye tell me then what force ye repose in the words imposed, and by commaundement, when ye oppose them against Christian freedome? Tell me also whether yee denie not that any Canons and constitutions made in Synods, in matters variable, are to be imposed by commandement: If they be, what is the reason that you Brownists when yee crie out against Church government as it is in England, speake in generall against Canons? And a little after in this your booke, ye denie all power of making lawes in things indifferent, terming it an adding to Gods word, and alleaging against it the extreame curse of God. I graunt the Churches power is limitted by the word in making such lawes: and so is the power of Princes. There hath béen much sayd alreadie touching the Lords Praier and other prescript formes in the Scriptures: but yet here come in newe reasons (if I may so call them) which are voide of reason. Houtos is the same that the Hebrew Coh, after this manner. I answere that this hath béen dealt in before, where ye must vnsay somewhat againe, or else the words of the Scripture now written are not the words of the Lord, but the like. Further, because Christ saith, when ye pray, if he willed we should say ouer ŷ words, then should we euer when we pray, say them. To this I answere, that respecting the rules for matters, when ye pray, when is as much as to say whensoeuer ye pray, because we may not depart from those matters conteined in the general petitions. But if we respect withall the prescript forme of words, there is a double consideration to be had: for in them selues they bee most excellent, perfect and full, and so brieflie do containe the whole summe and substance of all thinges which we ought to craue of God, as that nothing is wanting. But our mind is not able so largelie or vnto such depth at one instant to spread or extend it selfe in desire, as to bee mindfull of euery particular therein conteined. And also we are more moued, as seuerall matters of néede do presse vs to craue them particularlie. Hereupon it doth followe, that

as

52145

as on the one part, it were a great iniurie and hindrance that any man should binde vs, when any particular neede vrgeth, to begge reliefe onelie in the generall forme which includeth many things, and not suffer vs to expresse the very particulars and singulars: so on the other part, to binde vs alwaies in such sort to the seuerall particulars, that we may not at all vse the generals, is very absurd, and a disgrace to those most excellent petitions. For by this it must needes followe, that I may not say, Let thy Kingdome come: or forgiue vs our trespasses, as we forgiue them, that trespas against vs: vntil the Brownists disproue this, he is fully conuict. For if I may vse one petition of the generall heads when I pray, I may vse anie one; if any one, then all.

The next argument which is brought, is to this effect, that if we be cōmaunded to say those words, then should we sin in vsing any other forme, for those being in ỹ best forme, we are bound alwaies to bring the best sacrifice we haue, or els we are accursed. This reason I haue fully answered in that which went before, for I haue shewed in what respect, it is the most excellent & absolute forme, & the best, and can by no meanes, without great absurditie, yea wicked impie tie, be reiected: & withall what is necessarie and fit for vs.

Now for conclusion, let the Reader iudge, whether I haue more need to leaue of, as he saith, my popish dreames, or he his spirituall fantasies, I am farre from maintaining, that our Sauiour, or his Apostles did stint, or bynde men vnto certaine wordes which of necessitie they must vse, and none other: but this is the thing which the Brownistes must ioyne issue in with me. whether I may not pray saying, let thy kingdome come, or if I may so vse the prescript forme of wordes in one petition, whether I may not in any, and so in all? And heere let the Reader obserue that Maister Greenewood crying out for freedome, complayning of a tradition that bringeth our libertie into bondage, hee doth him selfe take away freedome, and woulde lay a bondage vpon men, and vpon the Churches. For it is to lay a yoake of bondage when men will restraine that which God hath

 left

left free to bee vsed, as shalbe most conuenient and profitable for edification, as to follow a prescript forme, or to reade
praying. Among the Iewes in the time of the Law, God
tied them to the Temple, and vnto certaine set howers for
the Euening and Morning sacrifice, but in this we are set
free in the Gospell. For I may lawfullie goe to the Temple to heare the word and to be partaker of the Sacraments
with the assemblie: and I may lawfullie frequent other
places, where the publike worship is. The Churches may
appoint the same howres for there meetings that were vnder the law, if it be conuenient, and they may appoint other
if it shalbe more fitte, hee that in these shall take away the
freedome which is giuen to the Churches, doth lay a yoake
of bondage. In like case prescript forme of prayer to vse
praying, being an helpe to the weake, and a thing sanctified
of God, and left free to the Church as neede shall require,
he that denieth that free vse, doth lay a yoake of bondage.
And so I charge Maister Greenewood here to doe.

In the next place there were three Arguments of Maister Greenewoods which I answered at once by denying
the assumptions, and shewing the reasons that moueth me,
for in déede, he setteth downe some propositions: and out of
them affirmeth that which is false, and so concludeth from
thence another falsehood. It is his whole manner of reasoning; if I set downe this proposition, God is a spirit, it is
most true: if I will now make such an assumption as this,
a bodelie substance cannot worship a spirite, this being most
false: there will followe a false conclusion, which is that no
man can worship God in bodie, he is now therefore to proue
his assumptions, and before he commeth to it, he crieth out,
stay and wonder, they are blinde and make blinde. Who
be blinde and make blinde the Brownists? This man hath
some great thing in his minde, which hee séeth and dooth
wonder, and now calleth vpon all other to stay, vntill hee
hath vttered it, and so to wonder with him. Is there anie
doctrine more spirituall (saieth hee) any more inculcated by
the holie Ghost, then this accesse to God in the mediation of
Christ

Christ, &c. I answer who dooth doubt of this? You confesse I will say the propositions bee true and waightie matters: which I doo in deed, and thereby doo acknowledge that praier is a spirituall and Heauenlie thing, farre from the power of man to performe of himselfe. Now Master Greenewood confessing I doo this, like as a great waue of the Sea commeth rowling and dooth in shew, threaten to ouerwhelme all, but sodainelie faileth of it selfe: So he swelling with the winde of his vanitie, crieth out stay and wonder, as if I should be ouer whelmed with the streame of his words, and by and by falleth of himselfe, confessing that I allow the propositions: which in deede include the excellencie of praier, and there is an end of his wonder. The first assumption, hee must proue is that to reade vpon the booke when one prayeth is a quenching the spirite; for this he alleageth the saying of Saint Paul, Quench not the Spirite, when he hath set downe this, he addeth that to suppresse and leaue vnuttered the passions of our own heart, by the work of the Spirite, giuing vs cause of praier, and in steed thereof to reade another mans writing, he dooth not doubt will be founde and iudged of all that haue spirituall eyes to see a quenching of that grace. I answer to this, that the speeches of the Scripture are most fit to vtter our passions by. And what haue yee brought, but the matter in question? If wee respect such as be not able so well to vtter: the spirituall eyes to see and iudge that to bee a quenching of the Spirite, are but the eyes of Brownists. Therefore all his beggarlie cauils which follow, and which haue been answered before, are to be let passe as they come.

The second assumption to bee prooued is that it is presumptuous ignorance to come with a booke. This is a lame sacrifice, because a man dooth knowe how to doe better and doth not; stil he would haue that graunted which is denied. For I say the booke is to helpe men to doo the better, which are in themselues dull, and full of wants, and without helpe should rather offer a lame sacrifice. The third is for striuing in praier, for which when hee hath spoken much of this striuing

uing which is not denied, for continuance and importuna-
cie; he imagineth that the whole matter is prooued, for this
as hee would make vs beléeue, cannot bee effected vnles the
Priest reade till he sweate againe, with vaine repetitions. I
might followe with many words in these and the rest: but
séeing he hath confessed, that the Psalmes were to bee sung
vnto God, let him shew how the verie reading then can bée
so grieuous a thing; for this the reader must consider, that
our question is not about the matter of prayer, nor any corruption by vaine repetitions or otherwise, nor about the hy-
pocrisie and vaine babling of such as pray but of fashion,
but simplie of the reading, when one prayeth: which vntill
he can prooue that diuers Psalmes either were not vttered
to God as praier, or that they did not reade them when they
did sing, he prooueth nothing, but deceiueth the simple with
the sight of true things which he spreadeth, and from which
he draweth foorth such false conclusions. I leaue to the reader but to compare his answeres he maketh to the rest touching these arguments, and see if they make any thing for
him, and not rather against him.

Argu. 7. The next Argument is that, We must pray as necessitie requireth: but stinted praiers cannot be as necessitie requireth.

Whereas I affirmed that there be things necessarie to
be prayed for at all times and of all men: which indéed are
the most things which wée are to begge of the Lord. Of
these there may bee prescript formes for all times: and for o-
ther things that fall out sildome the praier is to be applied
to the time, and necessitie. Here are large discourses and
such as this Replier doth much please himselfe in, as a
most spiritual man. This I take to be the drift of the whole
that in praying to GOD, wee must come with féeling our
wants, that so we may pray earnestlie, which I do yéeld vnto as an vndoubted trueth. He holdeth it as a great absurditie that we should want the same thing to morrow which
wee do to day, or that all congregations should néed the
same one day which they do another. Hee is most foolish in
this

this and such like obiections: for if I should stand to followe particulars, there bee fewe things which we may not either for our selues or for our brethren at all assemblies begge of the Lord. If there be speciall necessities, they are to be supplied. The matter is cleere, I will not spend time about it, more than I haue in my former booke.

But whereas the Brownist doth obiect, that a prescript forme doth shewe that men take vpon them to knowe mens secrets, which God alone doth knowe, it is most vaine and friuolous. The Scriptures doo shewe that we all stand in neede of the same thinges and euermore, being sicke of one disease, though there may be some particular cases wherein some haue their seuerall neede. And let him answer me now vnto this poynt: There be fiue or sixe hundred in one flock, which come together to pray; if it be as you would beare vs in hand, that there is such a variablenes in our needes, that to day our necessitie requireth one thing, to morrowe another: then euery particular man and woman hath seuerall wants, and is to pray for no more than they come with present feeling off, how then shall the Minister frame his praier to fit them all? One shall say, this pertaineth not to me, how shall I pray? Another shall say, this or that toucheth not my estate. Many shal complaine that their seueral wants are not touched. Tell me Ma. Greenwood, or any Brownist, doth ẏ Minister knowe what is in euery man? doth he know euerie man & womans particular wants? He is to make the praier in which they are al to ioyne wt him, in euerie request that he maketh. Or is your meaning ẏ euerie man and woman shall come vnto him before euerie assemblie, and make their state knowne what their seuerall neede is? Or can the Minister beare in minde when he hath heard? Ye may see into what absurdities blind fantasie doth cast men. Men are to pray for nothing but that which they feele the want of, and are prepared to aske, & are fit to receiue. For these (saith the Brownists) there can be no set forme. And I demaund whether the preacher doth know euery mans feeling, how they are prepared, & how fit to receiue? Will ye affirme this? or will ye confesse that these grosse fantasies which yet you will father vpon Gods spirit, doo quite ouerthrowe all publike prayer? For if it bee sinne for any to pray for more than he commeth with the present feeling off, if in the multitude the desires are seuerall, if it bee vnpossible for the Minister to knowe them, and how the hearts bee prepared and affected, how shall he make prayer for them all? how shall they all ioyne with him in euerie request? How much better is it to confesse that the most things which all are to pray for, and at all times are inuariable: and that men come not only to pray for that which they feele their neede in; but also to be stirred vp to pray for such things as either they thinke not of, or be dull in. I must needes here lament the state of our people which professe the Gospell, and cannot espie the grossenesse of these thinges. When the assemblies doo méet, and holie petitions are made which men haue heard at euery meeting, they ought to bee as feruent in praying as the first time they heard them. For it is a grosse wickednes in men not to bee moued with matter because they haue often heard it, but accompt it stale: as we see mans minde coueteth stil that which is newe. If men haue not feeling it is their fault.

Touching the faults in any Leiturgie, the question is not betweene vs, which reason what should be. That wh ch I spake of the preachers not limitted in their praiers, I meane the prayers before and after their Sermons which they conceiue. That our Sauiour prescribed no forme, I shewed the reason, that it is not a thing of necessitie, but to auoide inconuenience: neither are men tied to one forme in all churches. Against this the Brownist replying, biddeth me stand to this, and saith I will goe from it in the next argument. I say, all the Brownists vnder heauen shall neuer be able with force of reason to driue me from it. He first opposeth, that if I say it be at all times necessarie, then the Testament is not perfect. How can I say it is at all times necessarie, when I say it is not of necessitie? Christs Testament is most absolutelie perfect: but yet all things touching comelines, order, and conueniencie, which are variable and may bee changed, are

are not expreßelie mentioned. And that is one chiefe thing whereby the Brownists doo seduce many a simple man. For this Brownist doth confesse that there bee things contained in the generall rules of the Scripture, which are not expressed, but he will not haue any of those things variable, that is, such as may be for good cause altered. For thus he reasoneth, If it bee a part of Gods worship, and all times conuenient, then is it necessarie: and if it be not necessarie, put (saith he) such conueniencie in your cornered cappe, or surplesse. And a little after, but you graunt (saith he) it is not of necessitie, therefore it is not commanded in particular, nor conteined in any generall rule. Thus may we see, that he holdeth there is nothing in matters of conuenience or circumstance in Gods worship, which is not of necessitie. The ground of his reason is this: If it be either expressed in particular, or contained in any generall rule, it is commaunded of GOD, and man hath not authoritie to alter Gods commandement, therefore it is necessarie. I grant that matters of conueniencie are commaunded of GOD by the generall rules, and that men may not take authoritie ouer Gods commandement. I say therefore the Church doth sinne either of ignorance or of negligence, when it faileth in matters of circumstance which should serue for edification. But herein the Brownist sheweth himselfe most absurdly ignorant, that he will haue that which is commanded to be of necessitie at all times. For that he may not winde out here with shift, as his manner is when any grosse thing vttered by him is detected. Let the reader obserue his words, and he shall sée plainly he reasoneth for a necessitie at all times. For he saith, If it be a part of Gods worship, and at all times conuenient, then is it necessarie. And to manifest that he holdeth it all times conuenient: saying, if it be not necessarie, put such conueniencie into your cornered cappe. And againe hée ioyneth commanded in Gods word and necessarie at all times together. And a little after he saith, Whatsoeuer is commanded either in particular or in necessarie collection from the generall rules, are of necesitie to be obeyed, and not to be altered.

tered. This I note to stop his euasion: for many matters of circumstance seruing for conuenientie and order, are fit at some times in some places, and for some persons, and so by the commaundement of GOD then to be vsed, who willeth that all things be done comelie, in order, and to edification. Now, as the times do varie with the circumstances of place, of persons, and of other occasions, the same things which were conuenient may become inconuenient, and so not necessarie at all times, as the blinde Brownist dooth beare in hand, but to be altered. As for example, in the time of peace it is most conuenient that the assemblies should meete in some Temple or Church built for the purpose: the Church is then to ordeine that it may bee so. In the times of warre and cruell persecution when the enemies raunge about and rage: it may bee farre more safe for feare of intrapping, to meete in the woods, or secret places. Kneeling is the fittest gesture of the bodie when men in earnest prayer are to worship the Lord: the Church is to commaund it where it may fitlie be done: but if the assemblies be driuen to meet in such places as the ground being wet, and through the trampling of their feete doth become myrie, it is inconuenient that the multitude should bee compelled to kneele in the myre: and therefore the former ordinance is now changed. I might runne through a number of particulars, but these are sufficient to declare what a learned Deuine master Greenwood is, and how perfect a spirit doth guide his penne. He demandeth also full wiselp, whether wee doo not hold it of necessitie, seeing men are excommunicate, and deposed for not obseruing it: or as some verie ignorantlie vse to say, if it be a thing indifferent, why is it not left indifferent for men to vse or not to vse? I answere, that which is a thing indifferent, God commaundeth it shall be done when it is conuenient and for edification, and therefore when the Church doth appoynt or ordeine it, rightly he that breaketh it, wilfullie breaketh the commandement of God. And so on the other side, when it falleth out not to be conuenient, and the Church dooth alter it, hee that will now obserue it with a resisting mind, minde doth likewise offend against the rule of Gods word. I neuer doubted but that by necessary consequence it is to be drawen from the doctrine of the scriptures, that prayer is to be made before and after the word preached, but I speake of a commaundement in expresse wordes: therefore the places are cited here by the Brownist to no purpose. And all the rest of his words that follow are either in matters wherin we agree, or such as he collecteth from his owne ignorance, and which are answered before.

The next argument is, Read prayers were deuised by Antichrist and maintaine superstition and Idole ministerie, &c.

Here the Brownist, if he would at all speak to the purpose shoulde prooue that the very reading a prayer when one prayeth is the deuise of Antichrist, maintaineth superstitiõ & an Idole ministrie. But he flieth & dealeth about the matter of leiturgies, saying: he hath heard, the Pope woulde haue approoued ours, if it might be receiued in his name. If master Greenwoods newes from Rome were true which hee heard, the matter were not great, for the Pope will approoue the Lords prayer, the commaundements and articles of the faith, but he wil expound them as it pleaseth him. The Pope also to wind in himself, wil approue in shew many things which he misliketh, so they be not directly against his crowne and dignitie. And it is to be considered that the controuersies betweene vs and the Papists are not about the matters which we are to begge in prayer. There is no likelyhood that the Pope made such offer, because he knoweth we holde in the substance and grounds of the faith, that which quite ouerthroweth him: but if he did, men may see by these things which I haue noted, that master Greenwood doth but shift and trifle. He confesseth leiturgies were before Antichrist, and yet saith he was the deuiser. See the grauitie of this man: he is sore afraide that hee should here againe be said to condemne all Churches because they haue read prayer: and therfore he saith his arguments are falsely wrested. Answere your selfe then, and tell vs what ye holde

 them

them which receiue the deuise of Antichrist. Why crie yee not out of the marke of the beast? It is a pitifull thing to see in what a case the Brownist is: For he wil not cōdemne the Churches; and yet after he hath set foorth what leiturgie is, and affirmed that the new Testament is Christs leiturgie: he alleageth that they be accursed that adde thereto; and holdeth prescript forme of prayer an adding. Let him now be asked: is the curse layd vpon the true Churches? he will say no. Then prescript forme is either no adding to Christs Testament, or else they be vnder the curse that vse it. He saith leiturgies are another gospel. Then all Churches haue receiued another gosepl. The wordes that follow haue bin answered before. Where I sayd there would sundrie inconueniences growe for want of prescript forme of publike prayer. After he hath set downe that Christ is a perfect lawgiuer, and that the word of God is sufficient, he tearmeth it blasphemie to say there would be inconueniences without leiturgies: then all the Churches committe blasphemie, whether doe ye yet condemne them or not? This is from his grosenes which doth not se that Christs Testament is perfect, and yet there are things commaunded in generall rules which are variable, as I haue before shewed for circumstances of time, place, persons, sitting, kneeling, &c. He saith there can be no particular lawes made without breaking the lawe of God, as though the Church were not to see what in these is fit and conuenient vpon euerie occasion and time, and for that time to establish the same: But euerie man to doe as he shall like, or shal take the generall rule of order and decencie, for men will not agree: this is from rules of order to drawe confusion. Now this great deuine saith I haue made a faire hande in affirming leiturgies to be but a matter of order, or conuenientcie for edification. Seeing as hee saith, it is all the worship we haue: this commeth from him that hath the beautie of Sion, as he boasteth: which the inchaunters of Egipt cannot iudge of. This commeth from him that with his fellowes hath the cloude betweene them and vs, and the pillar

of

of fire before them as he speaketh in the next wordes. Because I say the prescript forme and the reading are but for order, he concludeth that I confesse the prayer is but a matter of order or conueniencie: ye say I haue made a faire hand. But I tell ye master Greenwood, if ye should goe into the Schooles and reason so in earnest, the young boyes would be readie to hisse ye foorth as a *non proficiens*, and howe faire hand should you make then? they will not beleeue ye haue it from your pillar of fire, but out of that dark cloud of your ignorance which is betweene your selfe and the light of the trueth. Now wheras I said, ý Church hath power to ordain according to the word of God, & to appoint such orders in matters of circumstance, about publike prayer, preaching of the worde, and administring of the Sacraments, as shall most fitly serue for edification: and then these orders being established by publike authoritie the discipline and censures of the Church are to driue men to the obseruation of the same that stubbornely break them. Here the poore Brownist layeth open himselfe againe to be as blinde as a beetle: he will needes haue it to be papisticall mudde, and that I am in an Apostacie. Because there can as (he saith) no other lawes be made in matters of circumstance, than Christ himselfe hath made: that to ordaine lawes in the Church is to plead for vnwritten verities: and to make the law of God vnsufficiēt. It is an adding to the word of God, which is execrable pride. All the Popes trinkets might bee brought in by the same ground. This is the foundation of Poperie, and Anabaptistrie, to giue libertie to make lawes in the worship of God. And by your iudgement which would haue men driuen to obserue them, our Sauiour Christ was an Anabaptisticall Schismatike that would not himselfe nor his disciples obey the traditions of the Elders. Thus speaketh this Brownist. But what beastlie ignorance doth he bewray and that in sundrie poynts? and with what horrible things in his blinde furie, doth he charge all Churches withall? For first when he saith that for matters of order and circumstance, there can be no other lawes made of them, thā Christ hath made: he seeth not the difference betweene the giuing

gene-

generall rules of charitie, of comelines, and order, which serue for edification that are to be followed in making lawes touching matters in themselues merely indifferent, and the very particular lawes thẽselues that are so to be made. Thẽ if it be true which he saith the matters of order and circumstance are not variable, but stand fixed as inuiolable lawes of Christ in the particulars to be obserued, which is false, seeing these circumstances are no part of Gods worship: As Paul saith, The Kingdome of God is not meate and drinke, &c. but as handmaids, to attend upon it, and to adorne it; and so are vsed and not vsed, as occasion serueth. I haue shewed this before in some particulars, as that the assemblies are in time of peace gathered in temples, and fixed places and open, in time of persecution and tumult in the fields, in woods, and secret places which they change, and at the commandement of the pastors and gouernours: the wise reader may consider the like not onelie for kneeling and such like, but in many other. And we sée that the Apostles themselues did decree some things for the time, which afterward were to bee altered, when the occasion was taken away, as namelie to auoide giuing offence to ye weak Iewes which stuck in the ceremonies of the lawe: they made this decree Act.15. That the gentiles should absteine from blood and from strangled. We doo not now obserue this decree of the Apostles, neither are we to obserue it, séeing the occasion is remoued for which it was made.

Furthermore, if there be no lawes to be made in matters of circumstance, how shal the flockes knowe what to follow or to obserue where the pastors shall dissent and varie in iudgement? Sall not some be rent into one part, and some into another? Now when hee saith this is to pleade for vnwritten verities, to make the Lawe of God vnsufficient, to adde to the word, alleaging those Scriptures, which shew how cursed a thing that is: hee dooth but ignorantlie abuse those Scriptures, and wickedlie seduce the simple sorte of men. For those Scriptures are against the adding of humaine precepts and lawes to be kept as parts of Gods wor-

ship,

ship, to binde the conscience, to seeke righteousnes, and the forgiuenes of sinnes, or the merite of eternall life in them, or against such rules of gouernement, as God hath set to bee perpetuall. This is against the perfection of the word, against Christian libertie, and in the chiefe things which concerne Gods worship, against the ground and foundation of our faith: and so a thing most detestable and accursed, which our sauiour also and his Apostles refused iustlie to obserue with the blinde Pharisies. But now where the Brownist hath his eyes so daseled with that pillar of fire which hee saieth they haue before them, that he cannot perceiue that to make and constitute lawes in matters of circumstance for comelines, and order according to the generall rules of the Scripture and not to binde the conscience, is no adding to the word, nor mixing Gods worship with mans inuentions, he is much to be pittied. And doubtles before this pillar of fire bee remooued, which is not the heauenlie light of Gods spirite, but a frantick presumption, by which the diuell doth delude men and blinde them with their swelling, he shall neuer see well. Some will say if these constitutions be not to binde the conscience of men, why are men forced to keepe them? Why should the discipline and censures of the Church driue men thereunto? In deede this is that which the freedome of the Brownists can at no hand indure. To answer this, the reader must consider what is the binding of the conscience. It is not to say simplie yee must for conscience sake doo it, or yee are bounde for conscience sake to doo it; for then all the humaine constitutions and lawes of princes may be saide to binde the conscience, because Saint Paul willeth to obey them for conscience Rom. 13. But by binding the conscience is meant, that such lawes are laid vpon the conscience to bee obserued as part of the worship of God: when men are punished for not keeping them as contemning Gods worship, then is the Christian libertie withstoode. But when ye discipline & censures of the Church, doo compel men to obserue the lawes, which in matters of comlines and order are made according to the rules of the Apostle: they are not punished for dooing or not doing the things themselues, but that by dooing that which is forbidden, or refusing to doo that which is commaunded, they disturb the peace, breede diuisions and offence, disobey where they are commanded obedience: these bee sinnes, and for these, men are to be punished. This is where the orders be, not against the word of God, but fitte for edification.

And now to conclude about this matter, all the Churches of God vnder heauen doe make such lawes, such Canons, and constitutions in matters of circumstance, and by their discipline compell both Ministers and people to obey the same. The Brownist alleageth against this, not only the sentences. Prouerbs. 30. vers. 5. 6. and Deut. 4. vers. 12. 32. but also, Reuela. 22. vers. 18. 19. Where the Lorde threatneth, that he that shall adde to the words of that Prophesie, he will put vpon him the Plagues written in that booke.

Tell me now Maister Greenewood, doe ye yet condemne all Churches? Ye do affirme that they which make anie lawes, doe adde to the worde of God, and alleage against them, that God will put vpon them the plagues written in that booke: which is a denouncing of the extreame wrath of God, for there is the lake of fire set foorth? If yee were not quite beside your selfe, how could you thus hurle your dartes of extreame condemnation, and strike all churches, and yet when I tell yee of it, crie out, that I am a lying Prophet, and will me to remember who is the father of vntrueths? But least I may seeme to father that vpon the Churches, which is farre from them, I wil note somewhat out of the harmonie of confessions Section. 17. The latter Heluetian confession saith, *Quod in Ecclesijs dispares inueniuntur ritus, nemo Ecclesias existimet ex eo esse dissidentes.* That there are vnlike rites or ceremonies found in the Churches, let no man iudge hereby, that the Churches dissent. And the confession of Bohemia hath, *Quare illi tantum ritus, illaque ceremoniæ bonæ seruari debent, quæ in populo Christiano vnicam & veram fidem, sincerúmq; cultum Dei,*

con-

concordium, charitatem, & veram atque Christianam seu religiosam pacem ædificant. Siue igitur, ab episcopis, siue a consilijs Ecclesiasticis, aut à quibuscumque auctoribus alijs extiterint, aut introductæ sint, de eo simpliciores laborare non debent, neque hoc moueri, aut perturbari: sed quia bona sunt ijs ad bonum vti. Wherefore those rites and those good ceremonies ought onelie to bee kept, which among the people of Christ doo edifie the onelie and true faith, and the sincere worship of God, concord, charitie, and the true and Christian or religious peace. Therefore whether they bee exstant, or brought in by the Bishops, or by the Counsels Ecclesiasticall, or by other authors whatsoeuer, the simpler sort are not to trouble themselues about that, neither with this to bee mooued or disquieted, but because they bee good, to vse them vnto that which is good. **And a little after,** *Et quanquam nostri, non omnes ritus æquè seruant cum alijs Ecclesijs, id quod & fieri non potest, & non est necesse fieri, vt omnibus in locis Christianorum conuentuum, vna & eadem ceremoniæ vsurpentur: non tamen vlli bonæ & piæ constitutioni repugnant, seseuè opponunt, neq; ita animati sunt vt ceremoniarum causa dissidia vlla commouere velint, etiamsi aliqua non admodum necessaria esse iudicarentur, modò Deo & cultui atque gloriæ huius non reperiantur contraria, & quæ veram in Iesum Christum fidem quæ sola iustitiam conciliat, non diminuant.* **That is to say,** And although our men do not equallie obserue all rites with other Churches, a thing which both cannot bee done, and is not necessarie to bee done, that in all places of the christian assemblies, one and the same ceremonies should bee vsed: yet they doo not repugne anie good constitution, or oppose themselues, neither are they so minded as that for the cause of ceremonies they will moue anie dissentions, although some might be iudged to be not altogether necessarie, so that they be not founde contrarie to God, to his worship and glorie, and which diminish not the true faith in Iesus Christ, which onelie dooth iustifie. **Againe a little after,** *Docentur & hoc agnoscere homines, traditiones humanas non complecti le-*

gem perpetuam & immutabilem, sed quemadmodum iustis de causis ab hominibus instituuntur, ita etiam iustis & grauibus de causis, & re ita postulante, violari, abrogari, atque mutari sine vllo peccato posse. That is, Men are taught also to acknowledge this, that humane traditions doo not conteine a perpetuall lawe and vnchangeable, but as for iust causes, they are ordeined by mẽ, so also for iust & waightie causes, & the matter so requiring, they may be violated, abrogated and changed without offending. The Augustine cõfession, *Querat igitur aliquis an vitam hanc hominũ, sine ordine, sine ritibus esse velimus? nequaquã, sed docemus pastores veros Ecclesiarum posse in Ecclesijs suis publicos ritus instituere:* That is, Some mã thẽ may demand whether we would haue this life of men to be without order, without ceremonies? In no wise. But we teach that the true pastors of the churches may in their churches ordeine publique rites or ceremonies.

I might set downe to the same effect out of the confessions of the other reformed Churches, but I will omit it as not necessarie, and onely note a fewe things out of Master Beza his Epistles. After he hath set downe Epist. 24. that things indifferent are so called, not that men may without exception doo or leaue vndone as often as they lust and as it shall please them and not sinne: but that they are so called, because a man may vse and not vse them well, and hee may vse them and not vse them euill. And moreouer, that things indifferent by themselues or otherwise, doo after a sort change their nature, when by some lawfull commaundement they are either commaunded or forbidden. And further, that the vse of them is generallie restrained by the lawe of charitie, and speciallie or more particularlie by constitution either politicke or ecclesiasticall. He addeth, *Etsi enim conscientias propriè solus deus ligat, tamen quatenus vel Magistratus, qui dei minister est, iudicat interesse reipublicæ, vt quippiam alioqui per se licitum non fiat: vel ecclesia ordinis & decori adeóque ædificationis rationem habens, leges aliquas de rebus medijs ritè condit: eiusmodi leges pijs omnino sunt obseruandæ, & eatenus conscientias ligant vt nemo sciens & prudens rebellandi animo*

nimo possit absq; peccato vel facere quæ ita prohib entur, vel omittere quæ sic præcipiuntur. That is to say, For although properlie God alone doth bind the consciences, yet so farre as either the Magistrate which is the minister of God, doth iudge it profitable for the Common-wealth that some thing should not be done, which otherwise of it self is lawful: or the Church hauing regard of order and comelines, & so of edification, doth rightlie make some lawes in matters indifferent: such lawes are in any wise to bee obserued of the godlie, and do so farre bind the conscience, that no man wittinglie and willinglie with a mind to rebel can without sinne, either doo the things which are so forbidden, or leaue vndone things so commanded.

What haue I said more than the Churches do hold, master Beza and all the most noble Instruments of GOD in these last daies, if I should stand to shewe it. Then ye may see when Master Greenwood doth so ragingly take on, and strike he knowes not whom, such furie is not fit for disputation in the Church. Let not the reader here suppose that I goe about to maintaine that the prayer of any is pleasing to God, which come with customarie words of course without feeling their wants: or that I should hold, that a set forme of prayer is of men to bee vttered without meditation and preparation, as many doo of an idle custome, as if the verie saying were a great seruice to God. Nor yet doo I hold that all men alike stand in néede of prescript forme in their priuate praiers, or that the feruencie of praier is not often times more vehement in vttering any request in priuate prayer without prescript forme than with it, if a man be able. I say further; A man is to cal vpõ God not only as his néed in any particular shal vrge him, euen at al times: but he is also to stir vp himselfe and to prepare himselfe to begge moe things than bee in his present feeling and memorie, which prescript formes are an help to direct him vnto. And when a man commeth to the publike assemblies to pray, the case is somewhat differing from making his priuate requests: for there he commeth not to craue those things alone which hee feeleth present neede of, or which hee is mooued withall, but to make common requests with the whole congregation, in all things that they are to craue. To this he must now frame himselfe: Among fiue or sixe hundred, the particular wants or desires are sundrie, one mooued more in one thing: another in another thing: soms come more fitter to pray, for this, and some for that. It is most certaine, that neither the prescipt forme, nor the preacher can see into these seuerall estates of mens mindes & consciences, or to the desires which they are most fit and prepared to expresse: neither is that so much to bee regarded, seeing that which should be fittest for one part, should not be so fit for another: but they must euery one frame himselfe to pray for al things which the assemblie doth pray for, which are necessarie to be praied for at al times and of all persons. Shall any man say, I am not prepared to begge these things, therefore they be not fit for me? Let him not be so wicked, but stirre vp himselfe rather to begge them with the congregation. Shall any be so foolish as to say, wee knowe these things before, I am not mooued with them, men for the most part do but repeat them of custome? Nay rather let him striue against such impietie, and say the things are not any thing the lesse precious which wee craue, because wee heare them often or knowe them before, or that many abuse them: and therefore we indeuour to begge them earnestlie with all faithful ones in the assemblie, seeing they bee such as are needfull to be praied for. In the rest I leaue the reader to compare his booke with my former.

The last Argument. The prayers of such Ministers and people as stand vnder a false gouernment are not acceptable. Those Ministers which stand subiect to the Bishops and their Courts, are subiect to a false gouernment and to Antichrist.

I did referre the answere of these to the third and fourth accusation: but yet I did take some exception, as my booke sheweth. The Brownist in replying here is in great distemper: I will let all his words passe, and come to the matter. I alleaged out of the Epistle to the Romanes Chapt. 7. that

S. Paul

S. Paule was held in some bondage, and therefore that Ierusalem from aboue is not in this world so free, but that she and all her children are in some spirituall bondage. At this he did crie out of Atheisme & carnal Libertinisme, affirming that S. Paule neuer continued captiue vnto sinne after regeneration, neither gaue place vnto euill thoughts. Where I haue iustly charged him with very foule matter, which now labouring to wash away, he doth bemire himselfe. First he crieth out of wrong in diuers things without any cause. Such as doo touch the question of gouernment and the blasts he bloweth that way, I doo here omit, because his fellowes doo make replie as he mentioneth vnto those things, and I must then answere. Onely I deale with him now touching the place to the Romanes. He willeth if I haue any common honestie, to let his former answer be seene. I promise ye it will be small to your credite and honestie let whosoeuer see it, seeing ye doo in shameles manner crie out of wresting and I knowe not what. Against my reason out of the words of Saint Paule, denie if ye haue the forehead, these to bee your words. And now (say you) that Scripture which the Apostle hath set downe in the anguish of his soule, concerning the inward strife of the flesh and the spirit, you shamefully peruert to your owne condemnation except you repent: for Paule neuer continued captiue vnto sinne after his regeneration, neither gaue place vnto euill thoughts. Paule speaketh there of the vnperfectnes of his owne righteousnes, which maketh the lawe deadlie vnto him. I will thinke you a fleshlie Libertine, if you recāt not this doctrine. What Atheist would thus haue defended his owne grosse sinnes? Thus farre go your wordes, and now let such as haue knowledge iudge what wrong I haue done ye. Let them looke vpon that which I haue published, and see whether I haue wrested your words, or set downe any vnsound poynt of doctrine as you would yet accuse me, and doo importunatelie crie out: but now your words are in the light, and your answere also which ye cannot vse such shifts to excuse. You lay open the disagreement betweene you and me. First you cannot agree

to

to this, that the regenerate may be sayd to stand in any bondage to sinne. You cannot conclude against it, but bring in another saying and so draw a conclusion: And that is, how I also affirme that one standing in bondage to open knowne sinne, may in that estate bee accepted and communicated with as the seruant of Christ by outward profession both at one instant: which is as to say, wee may bee to mans sight the seruant of the diuell, and the seruant of Christ both at one time by outward profession. So none should bee excommunicate, none without, the world and the Church, light and darknes, Christ and Belial, should bee mingled together. Well, then I aske this question both of your selfe and of your fellowes, whether there be any one of ye that can stand foorth and say, I see no sinne in my selfe; but so soone as I haue espied I ouercome and am not at all led by it. Tell me further, whether ye haue not this, that ye may say there is euil alwayes in ye which you cannot be rid of; and that doth holde ye fast and presse ye: Do ye not leaue the good vndone and commit euill, and such euil as is alwayes present in ye? Doe not ye find great sinnes that ye stand vnder as not able to come out of: If any Brownist shall deny he is such, or in this estate, he can be but a proud hypocrite. If yee confesse it, what doe you but confesse some bondage? Let me aske ye further, is there any of ye which dare stand foorth and say I am not a sinner in the sight of men? I stand not holden vnder any outward sinne: the Brownist must aunswere these questions, for he holdeth that men can not outwardly appeare sinners and be the seruants of Christ at one instant. What beastly geare is this? There is sinne that appeareth in the best men at al times, in gesture, in words, in deedes, in negligence, in wants, yea a thousand waies: who is able to indure ẏ trial of Gods law euen in that which outwardly doth appeare in him for an howre? And will yee cast foorth all in whome there appeareth sinne that he dooth abide in? The grose open sinners I confesse, which contemne and giue offence are to be cast foorth, but are those which abide within at any time free from open sinne? coue-
touisnes

tousnesse is a foule sinne, so is pride, selfe loue, and wrath. Doe all Brownists so fully shine in brightnes before men that in none of these nor any other they can bee discerned to be sinners? Doth all vertue shine forth in them? And touching that which I charged you withall, looke better now vpon your owne speech: If there bee any modestie in ye, it will be hard for ye to deny, but that I haue layde no more to your charge than your owne plaine wordes. For are not these wordes plaine, *Paule* neuer continued captiue vnto sinne after his regeneration, neither gaue place vnto euill thoughts? But now you make a protestation that you haue euer been free from such an heresie, and your last writing did testifie much. Touching your writing it was both last and first, except your bare argument; and there is no heede to take what ye say, for your matter commeth forth as the streame doth turne the wheele, euen vnto contrary motions. When before the rage of the streame turned the wheele to vtter the freedome of the Church, then it must bee in such perfection that the regenerate is not partly held captiue vnto sinne, nor giueth place vnto euill thoughts.

Now when the wheele must haue a contrarie motion to purge your selfe, there commeth as violent a streame that way. For here ye say, the children of God after regeneration may commit any sinne, except the sin against the holy ghost. And you also affirme that they may commit sin of presumption and obstinate sinne: In my iudgment you had neede of some fauourable exposition of your speech. The regenerate doubtles, as we haue examples in the scriptures may fall into grieuous sinnes, and doe through frailtie: but that it may be of presumption and obstinacie, you must declare how filthie incest is not the sinne against the holy ghost, nor if a man kill his Father, Mother, or Children. No more is witchcraft, and familiaritie with diuels. Is it your meaning, that the regenerate may of presumption and obstinacie committe these? If not, why doe you vtter such wordes and not make them plaine. I spake vpon the place to the Romaines, that the freedome of the Church in this world is but in parte and not perfect: he cried out, a fleshly libertie. If I should haue spoken as he speaketh here, what would he haue saide? But hee now he is afraide least while hee hath washed himselfe ouer cleane from Anabaptisme, he should ouerthrow Brownisme, as indeede he doth. And that is the cause whie hee tempereth his speech in the wordes following: that although in Gods sight obstinat sinners may be regenerate and so his children, yet not to men by outward profession: but are to be cast forth which I doe not denie; and then for the least bowing downe to a false gouernement, they are to be cast forth. This I omit as not the question betweene him and me, and leaue his words to be considered of the reader. But where he proceedeth in reasoning against me as if I held that obstinate grose sinners are not teo bee cast forth by excommunication: I maruaile from whence he can gather that. But let vs come to S. Paule againe, and see how master Greenwood excuseth his owne speech, and condemneth mine. It is out of doubt that as God is immortal & doth begette by immortal seede, as S. Peter speaketh: so all which are borne of GOD and haue therefore receiued the spirite of regeneration, can neuer loose that spirit. Whosoeuer is borne of God doth not committe sinne because his seede abideth in him: neither can he sinne because he is borne of God. 1. Iohn 3. v. 9. From hence master Greenwood holdeth himselfe cleersd, and may well say that S. Paule after regeneration stoode not in any bondage to sinne, nor gaue place vnto euill thoughts: because he euer repented, and the spirit of God in him did not, nor could not cōsent or giue place vnto sinne. His meaning then is this, that the regeneration which is from the spirite cannot be in bondage to sinne, and the graces of the spirite cannot consent or giue place vnto euill thoughts. This is most true, vnlesse a man will be so wicked as to holde that the grace of God may be in bondage and consent to the worke of the deuill. If this had been the matter in question betweene vs, and he had said no more, it could not be reprooued. But he proceedeth further and chargeth me with error, that when S. Paule reasoneth of the olde man, or corruption in him, I will needes cō-

clude

clude it of the new man, or inner man, or of the whole man. My wordes are extant in print, let all the Brownists scanne them, and see whether they can without falsehood and lying gather from them that I conclude that the new man or inner man which is ẏ grace of regeneration is in bondage to sin, or doth consent unto euill thoughts: the whole course of my wordes doth lay open the contrarie. For I shew how Paule touching the inner man consented to the law of God: And that in his minde, that is in the regeneration, he did serue the law of God. What is it then which maketh master Greenwood so boldlie to accuse, and so falsely? Euen the mother of headdy boldnes, and much falshood, palpable ignorance. For where I stand to affirme, that Paule a regenerate man stood yet in some captiuitie and bondage unto sinne. He doth imagine it will followe, that I affirme the regeneration to be in bondage unto sinne: because Paul is the whole man, and he that concludeth upon the whole, concludeth upon euerie part. In deede this is it which hath deceiued the Brownist, and by which he thus laboureth to seduce others: that where the Scripture calleth the regeneration, or the graces of the spirit, the new man and the inner man, (as it calleth the corruption of nature the olde man, and the bodie of sinne) he understandeth it, as though the person himselfe, who is regenerate were called the new man, or the inner man, which is farre wide: for the graces of the spirite, the worke of the spirite, the regeneration called the inner man, are one thing, and the man himselfe which is regenerat, another. The bodie and soule are Paul, the regeneration called the inner man, or the graces of the Spirite, are not Paul himselfe, but in Paul. The soule & bodie are Paul, the corruption through concupiscence called the olde man, is not Paul himselfe but is in Paul: because the regeneration shall neuer be extinguished the regenerate are reckoned and esteemed after it, not that the regeneration itselfe is, either the man or a part of the man. Dauid was a man regenerate, he committed adulterie, and murther, the soule and bodie of Dauid sinned, whole Dauid doth acknowledge himselfe a sinner, that is,

 he

he was a sinner both in bodie and soule: and yet the regeneration, the seede of God in him, the graces of the Spirite, which were as coles of fire for the time couered in the ashes, did not sinne, nor consent vnto euill thought. Paul a regenerate man, when he saith *Autos ego*, I my selfe in the minde serue the lawe of God, but in the flesh the lawe of sinne, calleth not the regeneration, I my selfe, but his soule and bodie which were Paul: then the bodie and soule of Paul in the minde, that is so farre as they were regenerate, did serue the lawe of God. The same bodie and soule of Paul in the flesh, that is in the corruption of nature remaining, because regeneration is not full and perfect, did serue the lawe of sinne: for he saith I my selfe for both. The flesh in this place is not Paul, nor no part of Paul, but the corruption of sinne spread ouer the bodie and soule of Paul. Euen so, the minde is not *Paul*, nor anie part of *Paul*, but the worke of Grace remaining, the soule and bodie of Paul.

Now the Brownist, not vnderstanding, but as the Apostle saith, They would be Doctors of the law, not knowing what they speake, nor whereof they affirme. 1. Timo, 1. would haue vs beleeue him, that *Paul* after regeneration was not in anie respect held captiue vnto sinne, nor gaue place vnto euill thoughts: because the grace of God in *Paul* was not in bondage vnto sinne nor consented.

Saint Paul saith, I my selfe in the flesh serue the law of sinne: which as I expounded in my former booke, doth not prooue that sinne did raigne, or that it is to be accounted such a seruice to sinne as is done on the other part to God, because this is by violent tyrannie against the will, so farre as the grace of regeneration hath reformed it; and the seruice to the lawe of God is with delight and willingnesse. This is the reason why he saith, It is no longer I, but the sinne that dwelleth in mee. It is not reckened his sinne before God, because hee doth hate it: but yet it sticketh fast both in his soule and bodie. It is no longer I that sinne: The Brownistes exposition is to this effect, It is no longer I that is the inner man, or the graces of the spirit that

doe

doe it, but sinne that dwelleth in me. Did the graces of regeneration euer commit sinne, or the inner man? If not, how can it be saide it is no longer I, for nothing can be said to do no longer, that hath not don before? And whē he saith, but sin that dwelleth in me, this in me, is not in the regeneratiō, for though sin dwel in man together with the works of grace, yet is it no fitte speech to say sinne dwelleth in the regeneration? Therefore this I, when he saith, it is no longer I that do it, is not the inner man, but the person of *Paul* consisting of soule and bodie. How fondly then doth Maister Greenewood affirme, that S. *Paul* in that place touching his bondage to sinne, speaketh but of that which is called the olde man? The olde man is the concupiscence and corruption of sinne. Where I alleaged that Paul saith, he saw a law in his members that did leade him captiue to the law of sinne, hee saith I falsefie the text: because it is leading me captiue, and not did leade me captiue. Paul speaketh in the time present, least he might seeme to speake of a former estate which he was not in then. And it was more effectuall to lay open the bondage to sinne, which in some respect the regenerate are in, though sinne haue not dominion ouer them, for him to say, at that instant holding me captiue, then to say did leaue me captiue. The cause why I put it in the time past is, that Paul is deliuered long since. The disciples sawe Iesus walking on the water, doe I falsefie the text, if I say they sawe Iesus did walke vpon the water? But this is not all, for this Brownist saith, holding him captiue, but it did not holde him. What can bee a more flatte contradiction than this? his reason is because there was a stronger, that suffered not the law in his members to raigne. The matter is not about a full dominion of sinne, but whether the body and soule were not so yoaked still with it, as to be forced to commit sinne. Now let me haue an answere to this, eyther from Maister Greenewood, or any other Brownist whether the regeneration be perfect in any. He will say I do hym

 great

great wrong to aske him such a question, because he professeth the contrarie. Well then, answere also whether the freedome of Gods children from sinne, while they liue here be perfect, or but in part, as the regeneration is? If ye will say the freedome is perfect, shew how there can be a perfect freedome from sinne, by a sanctification which is but a part. If yee say the freedome is but in part and unperfect, as ye must needes say, (vnlesse ye will bee right Anabaptists indeede) then tell me how it is possible, that where the freedome is but in part, that should be no bondage? For what is the imperfection of freedome, but that it taketh not away all bondage? looke how farre the freedome commeth short of perfection, so farre bondage doth remaine, chuse whether part ye will to affirme, eyther the freedome of Gods children from sinne while they liue here to be perfect, or else to be vnperfect. For if ye shall say the freedome is alreadie perfect, (as ye haue hetherto, by affirming that the regenerate are in no bondage to sinne) then shall ye continue in Anabaptistrie. If ye denie the freedome of the regenerate to be perfect as yet, (which in deede is the sound truth) then consider that howe much is wanting of perfect freedome, so much remaineth of that bondage to sinne, which as yet al stand vnder that line, and acknowledge your madnes in affirming so directly contrarie to the Scriptures, that *Paul* neuer continued captiue vnto sinne after regeneration, nor gaue place vnto euill thoughtes.

FINIS.